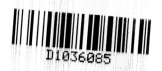

ACTIVE ENGAGEMENT

Also by Norman E. Amundson:

Amundson, N.E. *The Individual Style Survey*

Scissons, E.H.J & Amundson, N.E. *Straight Talk: The transactional analysis of communications*

Borgen, W.A. & Amundson, N.E. *The experience of unemployment*

Amundson, N.E. & Borgen, W.A. *At the controls: Charting a course through unemployment*

Borgen, W.A., Pollard, D., Amundson, N.E. & Westwood, M. *Employment groups: The counselling connection*

Amundson, N.E., Poehenll, G. & Smithson, S. *Employment counselling theory and strategies: A book of readings*

Amundson, N.E. & Poehnell, G. *Career Pathways*

Amundson, N.E. & Poehnell, G. *Career Pathways: Quick Trip*

ACTIVE ENGAGEMENT:

ENHANCING THE CAREER
COUNSELLING PROCESS

Norman E. Amundson, Ph.D.

University of British Columbia

Ergon
Communications

Canadian Cataloguing in Publication Data

Amundson, Norman E. (Norman Edmund), 1948-
    Active Engagement: enhancing the career counselling process

    Includes bibliographical references

    ISBN 0-9684345-0-9
    1. Vocational guidance. 2. Counselling. I. Ergon Communications.
II. Title

HF5381.A48 1998   331.7'02   C98-901107-0

Published by Ergon Communications
To order this book, *Career Pathways*, or other Ergon Communication publications, contact:
                Ergon Communications
                3260 Springford Ave.
                Richmond, B.C. V7E 1T9 Canada
                Fax. (604) 448-9025

Cover design and illustration by Gray Poehnell
Text design by Gray Poehnell

Printed and bound in Canada by Hignell Book Printing, 488 Burnell Street, Winnipeg, Manitoba, R3G 2B4; Tel. 204 784-1033; Fax. 204 774-4053

Dedicated to my parents, Norm and Jean,

who have always believed

that it was okay

to colour outside the lines.

Acknowledgments

In preparing this manuscript through all its phases, I have depended on feedback and support from my wife, Jeanette. Her creative insights and constructive comments are much appreciated.

Another person that I would like to acknowledge is Gray Poehnell for his technical writing efforts. He played a key role in layout and cover design and his creative direction deserves special recognition.

The foundation of counselling work upon which this book is based comes from years of counselling practice and supervisory involvement in a counselling centre supported jointly by the University of British Columbia and the New Westminster School District. I have appreciated the opportunity to work in such a fertile learning environment and would like to acknowledge the contributions of my colleagues and the many graduate students and clients who have come to the centre.

Table of Contents

CHAPTER *1*

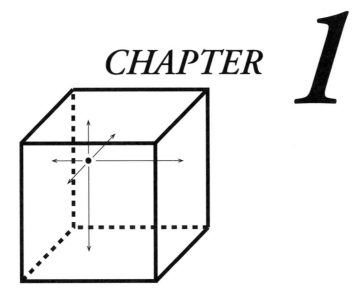

INTRODUCTION

As a counsellor educator I work with career as well as personal counselling in the context of a free community counselling clinic that also provides a base for counsellor training. In recent years I have begun asking myself the basic question "What is actually happening here?" whenever I find myself viewing counselling sessions (my own and others). This basic question has been fueled by a growing sense that much of the existing career counselling theory and practice has yet to adjust to new realities. I believe that it is time to view the career counselling process using a more active approach, an approach that I call active engagement.

Most people come to counselling with life problems that do not fall neatly into the categories of career or personal; life just does not define itself that neatly. Someone with a career problem will inevitably talk about their problem within the context of other issues and people. As an illustration, consider the case of a reformed drug addict who was having difficulty finding steady employment and came to the counselling centre for career counselling. Within the first session

I believe it is time to view the career counselling process using a more active approach

relationship problems, an unstable family background and anger management issues were added to the employment quest. In another case a woman with two small children decided to seek career counselling to assist her in returning to the work force. The problem was initially framed with respect to decision making between two options, starting her own business or working as a social worker for the government. Further exploration led to a discussion of her unstable marital relationship which played a major part in her consideration of career options. Even when people enter a counselling environment with seemingly well defined career issues there is a strong possibility that other issues will arise. This suggests that we must approach clients with a broader vision of the issues and also of counselling approaches. This integration of the personal with career has begun to be recognized by current career theorists such as Herr (1993, 1997).

In many respects sitting down with clients who have multiple problems can be an overwhelming experience. When I am faced with this challenge the question "What is actually happening here?" takes on even greater significance. Change happens one step at a time and often the most important step is the first one. I am convinced that the first step can be either in the personal or work domains; the reciprocal relationship between both areas will help to move the person forward.

The actual structure of the counselling sessions has been interesting to observe. A certain pattern seems to characterize most sessions. At the start there usually is a focus on relationship building and an attempt to define the problem. Most of the graduate students that I have worked with seemed to handle this phase with some confidence. This may be a reflection of their earlier training in the counselling approach as defined by Egan (1986). Communication skills such as paraphrasing, clarifying, empathy, questioning and summarizing seem to be effectively utilized.

After the initial counselling phase, however, many of the counsellor trainees were far less sure how to proceed. "So now what?" was the standard line as they faced the challenge of somehow coming to grips with the problems that confronted them. They realized that somehow they had to help their clients bridge the gap between the problem and a workable solution, while at the same time letting their clients assume responsibility for their own behaviour within a client-centred relationship. Making this transition proved frustrating for many trainees, and they found themselves locked in a pattern of continuous problem focused dialogue. As a supervisor within this context, I found myself increasingly encouraging students to become more creative and active in sessions by using techniques involving metaphors, drawings, in-depth exploration techniques, writing and poetry, solution-focused questions, behavioural rehearsal, and so on. Utilizing these type of strategies created a more "dynamic" atmosphere in the room and also seemed to facilitate resolution of client issues. I also encouraged more effective use of the "spaces" between sessions through practical homework activities which maintained the momentum, i.e. research through the internet, information interviewing, and networking. This more action-oriented approach is the primary focus of this book and will be expanded upon in subsequent chapters.

The emphasis on problem resolution that is described here is consistent with a view of the counsellor as "reframing agent." Clients usually come to counselling because they are "stuck." They feel the need to address a problem and have often taken some steps on their own, i.e. the very act of coming to counselling is one such action. As clients look upon problems (framing), they can't see how to find some form of resolution. In coming to counselling, they are seeking another opinion, another way of addressing a problem that appears impenetrable. Under these circumstances, it is not hard to see how many clients hope to have counsellors solve the problem for them. In most situations, however, counsellors resist the role of "expert" and work to facilitate a new perspective that allows for a more hopeful resolution of at least some aspect of the problem by using the internal resources of the person.

The process of resolving problems is very much associated with encouraging new perspectives and as such is dependent on the use of imagination and creativity. Counsellors in the system I am describing are encouraged to be creative and use their imagination to inspire clients toward developing new perspectives. Within this climate clients are encouraged to join with the counsellor in letting their imaginations work for them in problem solving. In addition to talking about problems, clients learn to apply their intuition and all of their senses to develop novel perspectives.

The application of creativity and imagination has also been extended to the very structures (conventions) in which counselling has been encapsulated. I have begun to challenge and change some of these structures to allow a more flexible and open counselling arrangement. These changes have included simple additions such as the inclusion of flip charts and felt pens in the room. Other changes focus on the counselling process itself. I am learning to leave space for reflective periods for the counsellor and the client within the counselling session. The timing of sessions has also been altered to allow for more flexible scheduling. These changes and others have helped to prepare a more receptive counselling structure for the broad array of counselling methods that are being implemented.

The activities associated with closure have been designed to recognize and celebrate the gains that have been made both in terms of personal insights and problem solving. Short- and long-term action plans are recognized as important elements in establishing closure. Attention has also been given to the affective domain and the feelings that are associated with counselling relationships. Feelings of uncertainty and loss are commonly tied to the process of ending.

Details related to the counselling processes and structures (Chapter Two) as well as the various counselling tasks (Chapters Three, Four, Five, Six, and Seven) will be elaborated upon in the material that follows. Also included at the end are some reflections on counsellor training and development (Chapter Eight). The counselling structure that is outlined is designed to be sufficiently elastic to incorporate a variety of practical strategies and techniques. What I have included within each chapter is a sample of the kinds of activities that can be used to enhance the counselling process.

CHAPTER 2

COUNSELLING PROCESSES AND STRUCTURES

Prior to illustrating the specific counselling tasks associated with the active engagement model, I think it is important to consider some basic foundational issues. These considerations help establish a supportive climate for the counselling structure that is being suggested. In this chapter I am addressing issues related to counselling conventions, relationships, goal setting, client needs, and communication skills.

Examining Counselling Conventions

In any form of interpersonal exchange, there are certain social conventions which set the rules and boundaries for the interaction. The history and purpose for the conventions often have been forgotten over time. Most people accept the conventions as a matter of course and would have to think hard to describe the rules of social exchange. To illustrate the place of social conventions in everyday life, think about what occurs when people socially visit one another during an evening. In this part of the world there often is an expectation that visitors will bring a small gift (likely a bottle of wine or some flowers). If the time has been set for 7:00 PM, it is usually fine to be a few minutes late (never early!). Depending on who you are visiting, there are certain expectations about which topics are acceptable for discussion and which are not; two

Increasingly I am asking questions and wondering how to restructure the conventions so that there is more room for the type of active counselling that I am proposing.

obvious sensitive areas are politics and religion. There are also guidelines about what food will be served, how much one should eat, how long to talk with any one person, when it is time to leave, and so on. Many of the conventions that we live by only become apparent when we enter into new situations and encounter people with different conventions.

The counselling relationship also has certain social conventions embedded within its parameters. Think of the ways in which people come to counselling, the ways in which they are greeted and made to feel welcome, and the length of time that is set aside for their visit. Think also about the physical structure of the counselling facility and the supplies that are readily available. What might be the expectations in the social exchange (in this case the counsellor and the client) and how might this differ with respect to gender, age, social class and cultural differences?

It also can be helpful to think of historical changes in social conventions. Imagine what it must have been like to walk into the office of Sigmund Freud or during the war years to visit a counselling office with an imposing desk separating counsellors from clients. Today, most counsellors have organized their office so that there are no external barriers in the room. As I look at the counselling rooms at one of our university training centres, I see two chairs facing one another in a small room with a small table on the side (primarily for the purpose of placing a small microphone). On one wall sits a one way mirror and there is one small picture on the wall.

For years I have just accepted the counselling space as defined along with many of the other unspoken counselling conventions. Increasingly I am asking questions and wondering how to restructure the conventions so that there is more room for the type of active counselling that I am proposing. Some of the already established conventions or assumptions that have come to my mind as I look at my situation are listed below (you may be aware of others):

1. Counselling is structured in chunks of time (in my case, one hour) with little room for flexibility.

2. There is an unstated assumption that the sessions will be primarily verbal in nature. There is no paper in the room or markers; and even if there were, there is no convenient working space. The size of the room also severely limits the amount of movement that is possible within the counselling space.

3. One room is available for "family sessions," it is larger and includes some toys for children. In the other rooms there is limited space and an assumption that the counselling will be primarily one-on-one. Bringing in a spouse or some other significant other is a special

circumstance which requires the scheduling of the family room. I remember watching a session during which the client unexpectedly brought his young daughter with him. Without the family room (which was booked), the counselling took on a somewhat comic flavour as the two adults tried to talk while the child was busy trying to stick her hand over her father's mouth.

4. Once a client and counsellor begin the counselling process within the room there is an unstated assumption that the dialogue will be continuous (allowing for some pauses). Interruptions have usually been reserved for special circumstances when there is a particular difficulty. Stopping the session midway through for a time of reflection or consultation is a new concept.

5. Leaving the counselling office to go for a walk in the park with a client seems to be associated with some degree of uncertainty. Liability is certainly one source of concern; however, it seems to me that the uncertainty extends beyond the issue of legal limits. Counselling is supposed to happen in the defined space that has been set aside for it.

6. Counselling appointments are booked weekly unless there are special circumstances. There is nothing special about the weekly meetings. Appointments can be more or less frequent depending on the need and the amount of work being done by clients outside the sessions.

7. There are unstated assumptions about the length of time that is necessary to do "good" counselling. It is usually assumed that more than a single session is necessary to achieve positive results. Even when the goal seems to be realized in a single session, there are pressures to schedule additional sessions. The point here is not that counselling can and should be done in a single session, but rather that single-session counselling should not be ruled out as impossible (Talmon, 1990). The corollary to this is that counsellors can often become more effective when they approach each session with high

levels of intensity, i.e. making the most out of the time that is available to them.

In painting this picture of social conventions, I do not want to come across as overly critical. Some conventions that I have not listed serve to further the type of counselling that I am proposing. For example, in our counselling centre the receptionist and coordinator are caring and personable and make each person feel welcome. Coffee, tea, hot chocolate and soup are available for everyone. The waiting room space is also spacious and comfortable. This structure clearly conveys a climate of "mattering." What I feel is needed, however, is a re-examination of all counselling conventions.

Having conventions is not the problem; the problem is not taking the time to examine how they impact the counselling direction that we wish to assume. A more active counselling approach calls for new conventions; otherwise we run the risk of "pouring new wine into old wineskins." Changing conventions starts with realizing the rules by which we operate; we can then begin to put in place the conventions we need to support what we are doing. I am taking steps to put in place conventions which are consistent with a counselling approach that values imagination, creativity and vitality.

> *A more active counselling approach calls for new conventions; otherwise we run the risk of "pouring new wine into old wineskins."*

With this focus on active engagement, there is the expectation that counsellors will be prepared to utilize a wide variety of strategies (art work, metaphors, movement, symbols) within the counselling situation. To open counsellors up to this possibility, I have encouraged them to have at hand the necessary materials for such activities and also to think broadly about such possibilities. Basically, counsellors need to be encouraged to use their full range of creativity and imagination and to do so with a full measure of intensity. Under these conditions clients will begin to reflect greater creativity and flexibility in their own problem solving (a necessary condition for client directed change). The intensity in sessions also communicates a certain message—"*this is a place where things get done and we are going to work hard to make the most of our time together in sessions and between sessions.*" When counsellors bring forward this type of expectation, there is an accountability that gets introduced into the counselling, i.e. "*we both need to work hard here.*"

Establishing
The Counselling Relationship

A good starting point for considering the counselling relationship is the work of Carl Rogers (1951, 1961, 1980). His development of the essential conditions of the counselling relationship are essential building blocks for most counselling theories. The three main conditions for the counselling relationship include genuineness, unconditional positive regard and empathic understanding.

Being **genuine** and **real** in the counselling relationship means putting aside the usual professional roles and addressing the other person with transparency and honesty. Connecting with the other person in a spirit of genuineness brings forward a congruence between actions, feelings and thoughts. The encounter between client and counsellor does not include any hidden agendas or defensive reactions. Spontaneity and sharing is encouraged on the part of both the counsellor and client. With genuineness comes the acceptance of imperfection. The counsellor does not have to hold tightly to the role of "expert" and, as such, is in a position to openly share moments of confusion and admit when mistakes have been made.

> *In considering the essential conditions for counselling, I think that it might be helpful to add "flexibility."*

Unconditional positive regard is closely aligned with concepts such as affirmation, respect, acceptance and caring. What is highlighted with this attitude is a willingness to accept the other person without judgment. Having unconditional positive regard means accepting clients as unique and worthwhile irrespective of their actions. It is possible for counsellors to accept clients and at the same time not approve of their behaviour. This distinction between behaviour and internal worth is an important concept to appreciate and it is also one of the concepts that is frequently misunderstood. With an attitude of unconditional acceptance counsellors reach out to clients with warmth and a strong belief in their ability to solve their own problems.

Empathic understanding is the attempt by counsellors to accurately perceive the experiential world (feelings and thoughts) of clients. The cues for understanding are found not only in language but also in the non-verbal and in the behavioural realm. Some situations are relatively easy to understand, while others require a more in-depth appreciation of underlying feelings. Often in counsellor training there is the implicit assumption that we all have empathy and it is only a matter of learning to express our understanding. I believe that the situation is a little more complicated; and while we all have some empathy, there also can be large individual differences. The source of empathy is difficult to ascertain, but theorists such as Schwalbe (1988) have pointed to factors such as experiences of powerlessness, contacts with others different from ourselves, and our relationships with others as factors important to the development of empathy (discussed further in Chapter Eight). There is little doubt that people assuming the counselling role require a strong sense of empathy. Beyond feeling the empathy, counsellors also need to learn how to express their feelings verbally and non-verbally. Expressing empathy requires risk taking and needs to be done with sensitivity and respect. Learning a formula such as "*You feel... because...*" is a starting point but needs to be taken much further. Often a hug at an appropriate moment can express far more than anything else.

As you consider these three essential conditions of counselling it is important not to lose sight of the fact that they are meant to knit together into an integrated whole. The following quotation by Rogers (at 84 years of age) as he reflects upon an earlier counselling session captures a sense of this integration:

I remember that as a very difficult interview for me, because she brought up things that I had not thought of a client bringing up. So I ask myself, "Can I be prepared for the unknown, for the unexpected, for something I didn't have any idea might come up? And can I be free of making judgments, can I hear whatever comes out and accept it as it is without making a judgment about it? And can I begin to catch the real flavour of what it is like to be my client at this moment? And can I accept the fact that almost certainly in the beginning I will make mistakes?" I will not understand quite correctly. Because I like to be able to accept the fact that I may make mistakes and then correct myself to get in real tune with the client. And not to be critical with myself if I do have a little difficulty in understanding just the exact meaning. And I guess the main thing I ask myself is, "Can I let myself go and really enter into this other person's world, just as this world exists for him or her?" And then one other thing occurs to me: This is only going to be a very brief interview of 15 minutes. "Can I be prepared for the fact that perhaps not much will happen, and also be prepared for the fact that sometimes in 15 minutes very significant things happen. In other words, I just want to be the maximum of flexibility and openness to whatever comes forth.
(Boy and Pine, 1990, pp. 143-144)

The words "flexibility" and "openness" capture in many respects the approach that is being suggested here. To attain this approach we all need to be willing to engage in careful self-examination. It is interesting to note the array of questions that Rogers asks himself as he prepares to handle what he considers to be a difficult interview. These questions reflect the previously described notions of genuineness, unconditional positive regard and empathy, and also a willingness to continually question what one is doing.

In considering the essential conditions for counselling, I think that it might be helpful to add a fourth dimension, namely **flexibility**. Certainly the notion of flexibility is in keeping with the spirit of what Rogers has suggested. It also reflects the necessity for adapting to a changing labour market and social landscape. Herr (1993, 1997) has indicated that counsellor flexibility is essential as we head toward the 21st Century. This flexibility is reflected through imagination and creativity and a willingness to be open to new situations.

Creating a Mattering Climate

Another way to look at the counselling relationship is in terms of the degree of "mattering" that is experienced in the contact between counsellor and client. Mattering has been defined by Schlossberg, Lynch and Chickering (1989) as the "beliefs people have, whether right or wrong, that they matter to someone else, that they are the object of someone else's attention, and that others care about them and appreciate them." When people feel that they do not matter in a situation, interpersonal connections are weakened and usually there is also some form of withdrawal.

Schlossberg, Lassalle and Golec (1988) have described mattering as occurring at several different levels. At the most basic level there is the need for **visibility**–having clients feel that someone recognizes their presence and that efforts are being made to ensure that they feel welcome. These efforts begin with the first contact and involve other office staff as well as the counsellor. In trying to communicate this concept to counsellor trainees, I ask them to think about what they would do if someone important was coming to visit them. What types of preparatory steps would be taken? In our counselling clinic people are welcomed at the front desk, escorted by their counsellor to the counselling room, offered a hot or cold drink, there is a place to put their coat, phone calls are not taken during the visiting period, and so on. Placing clients on the pedestal of "mattering" has some implications for entering the counselling room.

> *Mattering ... the "beliefs people have that they matter to someone else, that they are the object of someone else's attention, and that others care about them and appreciate them."*

The second level of mattering moves beyond attention giving to an expressed **valuing** of the other person. To communicate the importance of the other, it is essential to take time to listen to the problems that are being presented along with the underlying feelings. A unique aspect of counselling sessions is the fact that clients have the undivided attention of another person (the counsellor). The acronym **SOLER** is often used to describe the attending stance that is used by counsellors in individual career counselling.

S - squarely facing the client

0 - openness of posture

L - leaning forward (slightly)

E - eye contact

R - relaxed

The **SOLER** stance, embedded within an atmosphere of genuineness, unconditional positive regard and empathy, certainly communicates a valuing of the other person.

A third level of mattering occurs when clients have an opportunity to not only receive help but also to **offer help** to others. For many people, seeing themselves as having something to offer is a major step forward in terms of rebuilding self-confidence.

In a group counselling situation the opportunity to help other group members is readily available. For example, there may be ways to involve unemployed people more directly in the operations of employment centres. Perhaps a role could be found for them to work with staff and counsellors so that they could assume more responsibility for the services that are being provided.

The fourth and final level of mattering occurs when clients truly believe that they have established a **personal** as well as **professional**

relationship with their counsellors. In many ways this positive feeling is a natural consequence of responding to clients with empathy, genuineness, unconditional positive regard, and flexibility. This does not mean that personal friendship is established but rather a condition of personal caring that goes beyond the perceived boundaries of professionalism. With this level of connection, clients believe that counsellors care for them as people and are interested in following their progress over an extended period of time. Situations where follow-up is undertaken serve to reinforce the feeling of mattering.

Expressing mattering within counselling sessions is dependent somewhat on what else is happening for counsellors within the broader context. It is difficult to extend mattering to others when there are disruptions in either the office or in one's personal life. Under such conditions it is easy for counsellors to lose focus and become distracted.

The personal needs of counsellors form an integral part of the foundation for effective service delivery. In Appendix One there is a mattering scale that counsellors can use to assess the level of mattering they experience in their relationships with supervisors and others.

The general concept of mattering is applicable in many areas of life. As someone who travels a great deal, I often find myself in taxi cabs. In one memorable experience, I landed at a municipal airport and headed for my hotel in the downtown area in a taxi cab. Upon entering the car, I felt tired and sat back to relax and enjoy the ride through the city. Soon we found ourselves in a traffic jam and there is nothing like the sound of a ticking meter when we aren't moving to get my attention. Having lived in this city some years earlier, I knew the traffic patterns and realized that we could get around the impasse by taking a few side streets. From an assertiveness position, the first thing that came to my mind was to start giving directions. Since I had just finished writing a paper on mattering, however, I decided to try another tact. The taxi driver was from another culture, and I simply asked him where he was from (he was from Ethiopia) and how he liked the city. The conversation opened up and he quickly turned the car down a back lane while stating that he could get around this mess. Soon I was on the ride of my life and arrived at the hotel in record time. The price on the meter was $13 and he said that $10 would be fine. I wanted to give him $15 and the argument was on. That experience taught me a lesson that can be applied to relationships with taxi drivers and to many others. Perhaps if we spent more time helping one another feel that we matter, many of life's trials and tribulations could be set aside.

Finding Common Ground

When clients come for counselling, they are often quick to start talking about the "problem(s)." Prior to getting to the "business" of talking about the problem, however, it is often helpful to briefly engage them at a more personal level. Taking the time to find out more about their personal reality is a good way to establish rapport and also to learn some information which might prove helpful later in the counselling process. I have found that it is helpful to use principles from multicultural counselling when meeting each new client (Amundson, Westwood & Prefontaine, 1995). In some respects, regardless of the racial or cultural dynamics, each new situation is a multicultural exchange. The counsellor and client come from different "worlds," and it is important to spend some time focusing on both the similarities and differences (Pedersen, 1993, 1997).

Often the boundaries that counsellors draw between private and public topics for conversation are overly conservative and in no way reflect the willingness of clients to tell their stories.

Discussion during this initial phase should be framed as a form of "casual conversation" rather than some form of "interrogation." The essential conditions of genuineness, respect empathic understanding, and flexibility are integral to this process. From my experience I have observed a certain reluctance on the part of many counsellors to engage in more casual conversation with clients. Sometimes it is connected to a concern about being "professional," but more often it is tied to a personal view that they are being intrusive by asking certain types of questions. Often the boundaries that counsellors draw between private and public topics for conversation are overly conservative and in no way reflect the willingness of clients to tell their stories. Most people are quite willing to talk about themselves and, in fact, interpret this type of conversation as a reflection of "mattering." In situations where you might feel uncertain about asking a particular question, it is usually best to simply asking your clients directly about the appropriateness of the question. As long as questions are being asked in a spirit of good will and natural curiosity, there are usually few difficulties. When approaching clients in this way, I usually begin as follows:

> *"I'm glad you came today; before we get "down to business," I thought that we might take a few minutes to get to know one another a little. Is that OK? ... (If yes) perhaps you could tell me something about yourself, i.e. where you live, how long you've been there, how big is your family, what do you do in your spare time, and so on."*

While listening to the client describe his/her personal situation, I have found it helpful to interject at points where there seems to be some common ground. For example, a client may mention that they enjoy playing tennis and I would mention that I also enjoy this particular sport. Finding these connections strengthens relationships and also can serve as a resource when putting forward appropriate metaphors (to be expanded upon in Chapters Two and Five). The information that is generated can also prove useful at a later point in the interview when career exploration is well underway.

The principles underlying the notion of common ground can be employed in many situations where diversity is an issue. Cultural differences are certainly one important area, but one can also look to distinctions with respect to age, gender, disability, education level, religion, economic status, sexual orientation, and so on (Weinrach & Thomas, 1996). Differences in perspective need to be acknowledged, and at the same time you need to highlight areas of commonality.

Negotiating the Counselling Relationship

As the client and counsellor come together, there is a need to establish an agreement about the roles each will assume within this new relationship. Vahamottonen (1998) describes this process as one of negotiation where client and counsellor work together to develop an understanding of how they will proceed through each phase of the counselling process. The negotiation that might be undertaken is very much influenced by the perceived identities of everyone involved. The social nature of identity formation is described by Gilbert and Cooper (1985, p. 83) as follows: "our self conceptions hinge upon others' conceptions of us. In jointly constructing social reality, people mutually determine each other's identities – we become, in a sense, what others believe us to be." Thus, there is a mutual impact on one another, as client and counsellor seek to define their roles.

One practical reality which needs to be addressed right at the start is that of confidentiality. Clients need to know how counsellors are going to handle information about themselves and what will be discussed with others. In situations where others are involved in some form of supervisory or consultative capacity, this becomes particularly important. In some of the work that I have been doing recently, I have been applying the "reflective team" process as described by Anderson (1991). With this approach the client is informed that the counsellor will be consulting on occasions with other counsellors. Some observation (taped) is required and there are also occasions where the client has the opportunity to listen to other counsellors discuss his/her situation. In this situation a more communal form of counselling is undertaken where responsibility extends beyond the counsellor to the counselling team as a working group.

Turning to the actual counselling session, unemployed clients often feel invalidated as they proceed with their job search (Westwood & Ishiyama, 1991). Research by Borgen and Amundson (1987) has pointed to an "emotional roller coaster" that characterizes the unemployment experience for many people. Under these volatile conditions, counsellors might find themselves facing a challenging negotiation process with respect to the counselling relationship. Some people may be suspicious and wary of entering into a trusting relationship. Others may feel "beaten down" and hope that the counsellor will take charge and fix the problem. Whatever the starting point, counsellors need to be prepared to spend some time negotiating the nature of the counselling process.

As part of the negotiation process counsellors may need to educate clients about the many factors that are a part of choosing a career direction and point them towards a more collaborative relationship.

Many clients view career counsellors as having some form of "magical powers" (usually in the form of tests) that enable them to solve problems in short periods of time with minimum input on their part. As part of the negotiation process, counsellors may need to educate clients about the many factors that are a part of choosing a career direction and point them towards a more collaborative relationship. One of the tools that I have used in handling this discussion is the Wheel that is outlined in Figure One (Amundson, 1989a).

When I describe each of the elements in the Wheel, clients begin to appreciate the fact that counselling is a complex process requiring considerable input on their behalf. I usually make it clear right at the beginning that I am only able to provide an opinion after we have taken the time to gather some of the preliminary data. What usually happens is that the direction becomes clear to them through the exploration process and there is no real need for my opinion other than as a form of support or encouragement. During this time I try to clarify my expectations about the nature of the relationship, i.e. a desire for a collaborative approach.

Figure One: The Wheel

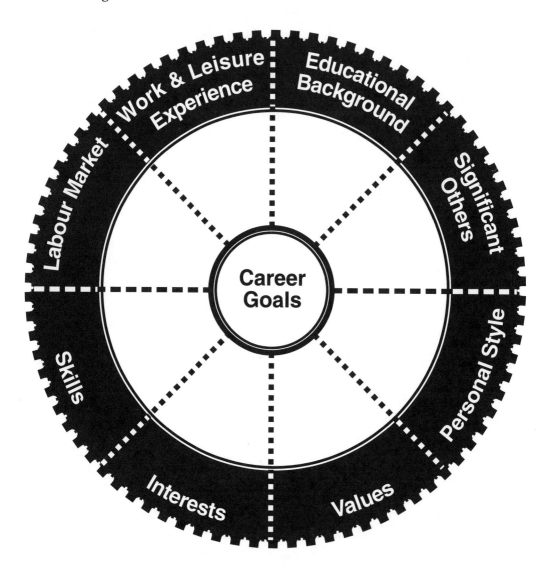

Clients who feel wary of career counsellors usually only come into counselling if there is some form of mandatory requirement. This certainly is not a very desirable beginning to counselling, but it does happen in some agencies; and if this is a reality, counsellors need to prepare themselves for this form of negotiation. Under these conditions it is usually helpful to begin by openly acknowledging the reluctance and some of the underlying feelings. Leaving space for clients to express feelings and concerns is important as is the counsellor's non-defensiveness stance to the viewpoints that are being expressed. Following the initial venting period, it is usually helpful to focus attention on the present relationship (immediacy) between client and counsellor and what might be profitably accomplished in the time together. What seems to work best is placing clients in the position where they have some choice over what is going to happen in the counselling sessions. They may have to come for counselling, but they can decide how that counselling will proceed. Giving clients this freedom is often the key to establishing a satisfactory working relationship. Having said this, however, it is also important to be willing to accept situations where clients will not participate. The old adage that you can take a horse to water, but you can't make it drink seems to apply here.

Negotiation can proceed at many different levels and in some instances there is need for re-negotiation (Amundson, 1994). Clients who are beginning to feel better about themselves may wish to change some of the conditions of the counselling process. In most cases, this expression of greater personal agency is welcomed by counsellors and is indicative of progress that is being made.

Negotiating roles and identity issues within the counselling relationship is, of course, only one aspect of the broader negotiation process that is occurring. Relationships in personal and working life may also be affected by the changes that are happening within the counselling situation. In an earlier article on negotiation, I described four factors (support from others; managing self talk; marketing; focused and persistent effort) which impacted the negotiation and re-negotiation process within the broader community (Amundson, 1994). Career counselling can help people to feel better about themselves, to develop strategies to control negative self talk, to learn how to market themselves to others, and to devise a systematic plan of action which has a greater likelihood of being successful.

Mutually Determining
Counselling Goals

The negotiation process that has been described also applies to the setting of goals for individual sessions and for the entire counselling process. Clients usually enter into counselling with some idea of what they hope to achieve. These objectives may or may not be realistic and appropriate for the counselling that is available. Both counsellors and clients come with perspectives, and it may be necessary to adjust the goals to fit with what is realistically possible. Walter and Peller (1992) provide the following guidelines concerning the development of goals:

1. Use positive language when describing what you hope to accomplish.

2. Describe goals using action verbs rather than nouns.

3. Focus on the immediate situation, i.e. what will happen after clients leave the counselling session.

4. Be specific and think through the details.

5. Emphasize the goals which are within the control of clients.

6. Use ordinary language when stating the goal(s).

Developing achievable and concrete goals is a process which is ongoing through each step of counselling. Collaboratively, client and counsellor work together to set a clear direction. When working with some clients, I have found it helpful to use a goal-attainment scaling procedure to help develop a fuller understanding (Cardillo & Choate, 1994). With this approach you ask clients to think about where they are now (base line; 0), what they can reasonably hope to achieve (+1) and what would be an ideal result (+2). Reversing the situation, what would likely happen if things got worse (-1) and what would be an absolute disaster (-2). To illustrate this process, consider the case of a 33 year old single man who was working in an organization that was in the midst of downsizing. At the time of counselling the client was unsure about whether to start looking for other employment or stay with his current organization (base line; 0). As he looked at his goals, he could see that what he was hoping to get from the counselling was some guidance about what decision to make. He realized that the decision was his to make but he wanted some additional information on which to base his decision (+1). The ideal, from his perspective, was a clear statement from the counsellor about what he should do next (+2). Seen from the negative stance, he was hoping that he wouldn't be even more confused following his visit to the counsellor (-1) and the absolute disaster scenario (-2) was one in which he made the wrong decision. In this instance the goals themselves became the focus for discussion and change. Two major issues for consideration were responsibility and the need to accept an uncertain labour market. The concept of "positive uncertainty" was very important here. along with an emphasis on personal agency (discussed in more detail in Chapter Six).

Collaboratively, client and counsellor work together to set a clear direction.

The successful setting and realization of goals by clients requires close attention to personal motivation and to environmental constraints. Flexibility and persistence is necessary in many situations, and clients must be prepared to make the necessary adjustments in the face of difficult situations. You can help clients prepare for challenging situations by offering support (encouragement and follow-up) and guidance (contemplative and practical).

Coping with Client Reluctance

The desire of counsellors to help clients is not always reciprocated and in some situations counsellors run the risk of getting themselves into a "game triangle" situation. In the game triangle, counsellors start out with enthusiasm and a desire to rescue their clients. Unfortunately some clients do not perform up to expectations and ultimately the rescue efforts are unsuccessful. This leads to frustration and a tendency to become persecutors rather than rescuers as counsellors attempt "forced rescues." The end result is that most rescue attempts fail under these conditions and counsellors end up as the victims.

Clients who are not working hard in sessions or between sessions are sending a message. Either the counsellor is running too far ahead of them or they are simply not motivated at the present time.

Avoiding game triangles while maintaining an appropriate level of intensity can be challenging. Nevertheless, it is a position that counsellors must cultivate for themselves. Being intense must be balanced with a respect for how clients can solve their own problems. Clients who are not working hard in sessions or between sessions are sending a message. Either the counsellor is running too far ahead of them or they are simply not motivated at the present time.

Understanding the sources of reluctance is an important starting point for dealing with difficult client situations (Amundson & Kenney, 1979). Five common sources are briefly described below:

1. Fear of the Unfamiliar

Many clients are hesitant to see a counsellor because they have little or no experience with this type of relationship. They may have some misperceptions about what happens in a counselling session and this can interfere with the counselling process. In some instances they might believe that counsellors are similar to magicians–they have a special test that will tell them all that they need to know. Others may worry about what they might have to divulge and the degree of confidentiality that will be maintained. Feeling insecure in a new situation is a natural reaction, and counsellors under these conditions need to discuss fully the counselling process and build rapport with their clients.

2. Refusal to Acknowledge the Problem and/or Take Responsibility for the Problem

Coming to counselling can be a difficult step because of some of the societal fears about "being crazy" or "being responsible" for problems. Seeking assistance can be viewed as a sign of personal weakness in a society where strength and independence are highly valued. Career counselling has some advantages in that it is more socially acceptable than personal counselling, but it still carries some misperceptions with it. Also, many people use the guise of career counselling when they are seeking help with personal problems. Within this context it is not surprising that clients may have some difficulty acknowledging problems and their personal responsibilities for the issues they are facing. This does not mean that clients need to bear the total burden of responsibility for difficult situations; there certainly are many examples of unjust firings and so on. What is necessary is that they are willing to assess realistically both themselves and the external environment.

3. Job Loss / Job Search Burnout

Research conducted with my colleague Bill Borgen has indicated that in many instances the experience of unemployment can be regarded as an emotional roller coaster (Borgen & Amundson, 1987). Contained within this experience are feelings of loss (shock, anger, worry, anxiety) and burnout (discouragement, stagnation, anger, desperation, fear). Under these changing emotional conditions, clients may appear unmotivated and resentful. Taking time to acknowledge these reactions and to normalize the situation can help to reduce any apparent reluctance.

4. Client versus the System

Many clients have had negative relationships with various government and educational institutions. These prior experiences with the "system" influence the way in which they will approach counsellors, particularly those counsellors in another bureaucracy. Under these conditions it is easy to be put on the defensive. Rather than responding to a barrage of criticisms, I have found it helpful to allow some time for venting, to acknowledge the hurt feelings and to look ahead to what can be accomplished in the present situation.

5. Secondary Gains

Some clients may view counselling as a threat to the financial assistance (unemployment benefits, social assistance, support payments) they are currently receiving. Particularly in cases where they are directed into counselling situations, they may be reluctant to discuss their situations openly. It is important that counsellors clarify these dynamics in the initial discussion; otherwise they may find themselves frustrated and confused by the ensuing interpersonal reactions.

Understanding the sources of reluctance can be an important first step toward working with reluctant client behaviours. In addition, counsellors also need to understand how their reactions might be supporting and in some cases encouraging reluctance.

Coping with reluctance requires patience, empathy, clear communication and non-defensiveness, as well as a willingness to make referrals when this seems necessary. Bezanson, DeCoff and Stewart (1996) suggest that to deal with reluctance, counsellors need to do the following: a. manage their own reactions to reluctant behaviour; b. create counselling conditions of safety and clarity for clients; c. create counselling conditions which motivate clients; and d. apply specific counselling coping skills (acknowledge reluctance, involve clients in re-assessing goals, involve clients in assessing risks, and use appropriate confrontation strategies).

I think that it is also important to state at this point that counsellors may not be able to engage all clients in meaningful counselling relationships. There are some people that are just not ready for counselling. It is important to know when to step aside and openly acknowledge that the situation is not working (make referrals when this is warranted). Counsellors are only one part of the helping equation; and without client cooperation, little can be accomplished.

Learning to work with reluctance can be a challenging task, but it also can be a source of great satisfaction. It is often the difficult clients that "push the buttons of the counsellor" and test the limits of counselling abilities. As counsellors successfully work within challenging situations, new counselling skills are developed and refined and self-confidence grows. Within this context, counsellors are more prepared to be innovative and flexible and to accept the challenges of the active engagement counselling approach.

Applying Communication Skills

This chapter has focused on a number of important tasks relevant to the establishment of a positive working relationship. Meeting this objective requires the use of good communication skills. When describing a set of communication skills, it is important to acknowledge that there are many different ways of organizing skills. The communication skill set described below is adapted from the skills presented in the group counselling training program developed through Human Resources Development Canada (Borgen, Pollard, Amundson & Westwood, 1989). A short definition and illustration for each skill area will be provided along with an illustration.

1. Paraphrasing

When using this skill, you are putting into your own words the message that you are receiving from the other person (not parroting). The emphasis in paraphrasing is upon the content of the message.

Illustration: *"If I understand you correctly, you would like to spend some time today practising for your interview scheduled for tomorrow."*

2. Clarifying

There may be situations where you need to check (ask specific questions) to see that you have understood the situation correctly. In communicating this concern, you describe what you have heard, state your confusion and look to the other person for clarification.

Illustration: *"When you were describing your last job, I wasn't sure whether you enjoyed working at the mill or if you really wanted to find something else?"*

3. **Primary Empathy**

Primary empathy is an extension of paraphrasing. With empathy you are reflecting the feelings as well as the content. The formula that is often used is: "*You feel ... because ....*" It is important with empathy that you vary the form of your statements (don't overuse the formula) so that you do not appear stilted.

> Illustration: "*It's upsetting when someone doesn't let you explain what you meant.*"

4. **Summarizing**

When summarizing, you are pulling together, organizing, and integrating the major points that have been made. This serves as a conclusion, a perception check and a means of making a transition from one topic to another.

> Illustration: "*Let me see if I have this straight. You weren't able to make the phone calls you intended because of telephone problems and a lack of sleep.*"

5. **Information Giving**

With information giving, you are providing specific information in a clear, non-threatening and succinct fashion. Also covered under this skill are situations where there is a need to advise people how to obtain additional information.

> Illustration: "*I have information about that particular college that I could show you. You might also use the computer in the library to explore other possibilities.*"

6. Moderating

Through moderating you are ensuring that all sides of an issue are explored. In a group context you are encouraging everyone to express their opinions.

> Illustration: "*We've spent a lot of time talking about the advantages of going back to school. I wonder if there are any potential difficulties that you might face.*"

7. Linking

You use the linking skill to illustrate similarities and differences of opinion between various people. You can also show how different ideas can be related.

> Illustration: "*You tend to be leaning toward the computer field, but your parents would like you to consider medicine.*"

8. Blocking

During an interview you may find that there are times when it is necessary to stop undesirable, unethical, or inappropriate actions. When using blocking, you may find it helpful to ensure that your words are consistent with your body language.

> Illustration: Counsellor raising hand slightly. "*I can see that you are upset, but when you are yelling it is hard to talk with you. Please change the tone of your voice.*"

9. Supporting

The supporting skill involves encouraging and praising others. In supporting others, it is helpful to be as specific as possible when making positive statements.

Illustration: "*That was terrific. I really liked the way you interjected that question at the beginning of our practice interview.*"

10. Limiting

Limiting is a skill that you use when defining boundaries and setting limits for clients. One of the differences between blocking and limiting is that when you are limiting there often is the implication that you are stopping something for the moment but you will be returning later.

Illustration: "*I can see that you are excited about this new idea, but I wonder if we could go over the homework assignment before we move in a different direction. Let's set ourselves 15 minutes to review the homework and then we can try some of these other ideas.*"

11. Consensus Taking

Consensus taking emphasizes the need for full agreement before initiating action. With consensus taking, it is important not to interpret silence as consent; the question still needs to be asked.

Illustration: "*Before we go on I just want to make sure that you agree fully with the plan that is before us.*"

12. Open-ended Questioning

When using open-ended questioning, you are enquiring in a manner that encourages the other person to reflect and expand their thinking. It is not usually helpful to ask "why" questions at the start since the answers may require insight into situations that clients don't yet have.

Illustration: "*What were your thoughts and feelings when you learned that the course won't be offered until next year?*"

13. Advanced Empathy

With advanced empathy, you are communicating an understanding of feelings and experiences that are implied rather than being expressed directly. The focus is on issues which are not being acknowledged, such as intentions, wishes, fears, and needs.

Illustration: "*At one level you seem confident about making those cold calls, but I'm also picking up some hesitancy. It's a scary job to start telephoning people you don't know.*"

14. Strength Challenge

Strength challenge is based on the notion of challenging clients with their strengths rather than their failures. The emphasis is on specific behaviours or attitudes which are being denied; but which, from your observations, are present. Many people will undersell themselves and they need to be reminded (with specific behavioural observations) of the strengths that they do possess.

> *Strength challenge is based on the notion of challenging clients with their strengths rather than their failures.*

Illustration: "*You've indicated that you can't think on your feet quickly, but from what I've observed in the previous activity, you seem able to handle yourself very well under pressure. When I asked you that question that wasn't in the book, you took your time and gave me quite a good response.*"

15. Confrontation

With confrontation, you are challenging clients with inconsistencies in their behaviour or attitudes. Usually, this is presented as a question rather than a statement, and it should be used sparingly.

> Illustration: "*In our last session you seemed keen to get this workbook so that you could do some of the exercises. Today I notice that you haven't started on any of the exercises; I'm wondering what's happening here?*"

16. Immediacy

Immediacy involves discussing directly and openly with another person about what is happening in the present relationship. Communication may be taking place at various levels and there is an attempt to focus on the underlying dynamics.

> Illustration: "*I notice that you seem really uncomfortable in the practice session. I'm wondering if there is something about what I am doing today that is contributing to this feeling?*"

17. Self-Disclosure

Through self-disclosure, you share your own personal experiences with others. Self-disclosure can be helpful in releasing underlying emotions (anger, fear, etc.) that are not being acknowledged but may be preventing the client from moving on. In making disclosures, you must be genuine and sensitive to the amount and depth of personal revelation appropriate to the situation.

> Illustration: "*Hearing you talk about being locked out, reminds me of some of my experiences a few years back. Like you, I was totally devastated by the lack of concern that was being expressed.*" (Linking and Self-Disclosure)

18. Process Observing

With process observing, there is reflection and a verbal description of the dynamics of the counselling process that have been observed over a period of time.

Illustration: *"I'm really enjoying your smile today. As I think back to how you were feeling when you first came here, I can't believe how much you've changed."*

One final communication skill which is often overlooked is that of HUMOUR. An ability to laugh at oneself and at some of the difficult situations in life can be a wonderful gift. The use of appropriate humour can help to build relationships and reduce tension. Humour can take many forms. Some people are able to twist situations to see the humorous side; others rely on a more structured approach. One example of humour in an employment context that I recently came across was on the internet (Riley Guide, www.dbm.com/jobguide/). This letter is of unknown origins, but was apparently sent to a university department head following receipt of a rejection letter (the names are of course fictitious).

> *An ability to laugh at oneself and at some of the difficult situations in life can be a wonderful gift.*

Dear Professor Hombre:

Thank you for your letter of March 6. After careful consideration, I regret to inform you that I am unable to accept your refusal to offer me an assistant professor position in your department.

This year I have been particularly fortunate in receiving an unusually large number of rejection letters.

With such a varied and promising field of candidates, it is impossible for me to accept all refusals.

Despite the University of Towanda's outstanding qualifications and previous experience in rejecting applicants, I find that your rejection does not meet my needs at this time. Therefore, I will assume the position of assistant professor in your department this May. I look forward to seeing you then.

Best luck in rejecting future applications.

Sincerely,

Goddard Youville

Applying the communication skills that have been described here requires ongoing practice and an openness to constructive feedback. The skills that have been presented in this section represent a broad range of communications skills. These skills can be utilized through all levels of the counselling process, i.e. applied in problem defining tasks, problem resolving tasks, and in closure. The skills, while presented in isolation here, are often applied in complex constellations by experienced and well-trained counsellors. Chapter Eight describes some of the issues associated with the development of good counselling skills and strategies.

Summary

The ideas presented to this point are important in setting a context for career counselling. Counselling conventions need to be challenged and restructured to allow greater imagination and creativity in counselling sessions. The actual delivery of counselling depends on the establishment of positive and well-defined counselling relationships where expectations and goals are clearly articulated. The establishment of positive relationships depends on many factors and can be challenging at times. Nevertheless, it is possible in most instances to establish a constructive counselling climate by understanding the dynamics of client reluctance and by developing and applying a broad range of communication skills.

The focus now shifts from counselling processes and structures to the actual counselling tasks that serve to define career counselling. These tasks begin with problem defining issues, move through problem resolution and end with closure.

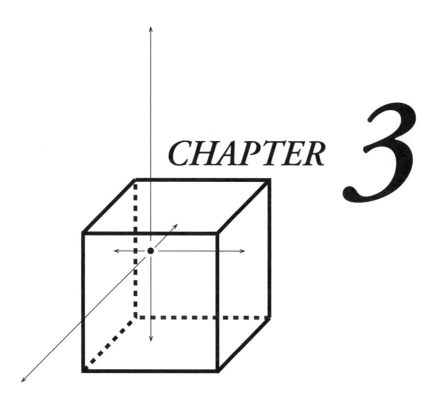

CHAPTER 3

PROBLEM
DEFINING
TASKS

As I mentioned at the end of the last chapter, the focus shifts at this point from describing foundational counselling processes and structures to describing in practical terms the tasks associated with the active engagement career counselling model. These tasks have been organized with respect to defining, resolving and closing issues. The first of these series of tasks, the ones addressed in this chapter, focus on how clients define their problems and the counselling process. As counsellors, we need to provide clients with the opportunity to fully describe their situation and to discuss how we might work together to bring about some form of resolution.

Stating the Problem and Setting Expectations

In situations where clients come voluntarily for counselling the initial statement of the problem is quite straightforward and in most instances follows smoothly after the preliminary "welcoming scenario," i.e. casual conversation, asking people about themselves, and so on. Upon sitting down in the counselling room, most clients soon begin to talk about their problem(s). In situations where there is silence or awkwardness, counsellors may initiate the discussion by using a question such as the following: *"So, what brings you here today?"* This question is intended to move the conversation from rapport building to a more direct focus on the problem. Responses to this enquiry may vary considerably. Some clients will state the problem in a clear fashion, while others may be very global or have two or three different issues which might run together.

I have found it helpful at this point to just accept the problem as stated and then move to a discussion of the expectations that clients have with respect to problem resolution and to the nature of the counselling relationship. Questions such as the following help to initiate this dialogue: *"What specifically are you hoping to achieve in our sessions? How do you see us working together to accomplish the tasks that you have described?"* The discussion here focuses on a negotiation process about roles within the counselling relationship. The section on "Negotiating the Counselling Relationship" in the previous chapter elaborates many of the issues of concern.

> *In instances where the focus isn't clear you may need to spend some time helping clients become specific about what they are hoping to achieve.*

Following the discussion of expectations, there is a return to the problem(s) that were initially put forth. In instances where the focus isn't clear, you may need to spend some time helping clients become specific about what they are hoping to achieve. When there is more than one issue, clients may need to separate their problems and rank order them in terms of importance. Achieving this clarity requires the use of communication skills such as paraphrasing, clarifying, empathy, moderating, and summarizing.

Patsula (1992) suggests as part of a preliminary assessment process that you try at this point to understand your client's problem by helping him/her to formulate constraint statements. A constraint statement is one in which the client states both the difficulty and reason for the problem. Some examples of constraint statements are listed below:

> *"I can't find a job because the plant is closed and there is no work in this area."*

> *"I need to take the computer course so that I can qualify for more receptionist jobs"*

> *"I don't know where to begin my job search because I don't have a clear career direction"*

To help clients specify their constraint statements, you can introduce a summary statement focusing on the issue of concern. Using the first example listed above, you might respond as follows:

> *"So as you see it, you can't find a job because of the plant closing and the fact that there just isn't any similar work in this area."*

The client's response to the summary statement will either be agreement or clarification.

As part of the problem clarification process, I have found it helpful to use the employability dimensions as described by Human Resources Development Canada. According to this system, clients typically seek assistance with the following tasks:

1. career exploration and decision making,

2. occupational or generic skill development,

3. job search techniques, and

4. job maintenance skills

Some clients will be focused in one area, while others will find themselves facing more wide-ranging challenges. Clients can identify their issues using the metaphor of a roadmap (see Figure Two from the Starting Points program, Borgen & Amundson, 1996). As clients move toward a new job, they face various challenges (roadblocks); but they also can overcome problems by participating in activities illustrated in the stopover positions of the figure. Incidentally, although this roadmap appears linear, it is possible for clients to be working at more than one roadblock at the same time.

The roadmap illustration is a useful metaphor since four of the roadblocks are consistent with the employability dimensions. An additional roadblock has been added at the beginning—one which refers to situations where clients are unsure about their readiness to begin the process. This uncertainty may be a reflection of alcohol or drug abuse, daycare problems, or many other issues.

If you turn now to a more complicated situation, the reality for many counselling professionals is that they must face the challenge of working with clients who are required to come for counselling. Under these circumstances a preliminary discussion of the issue of forced participation

Figure Two: The Roadmap

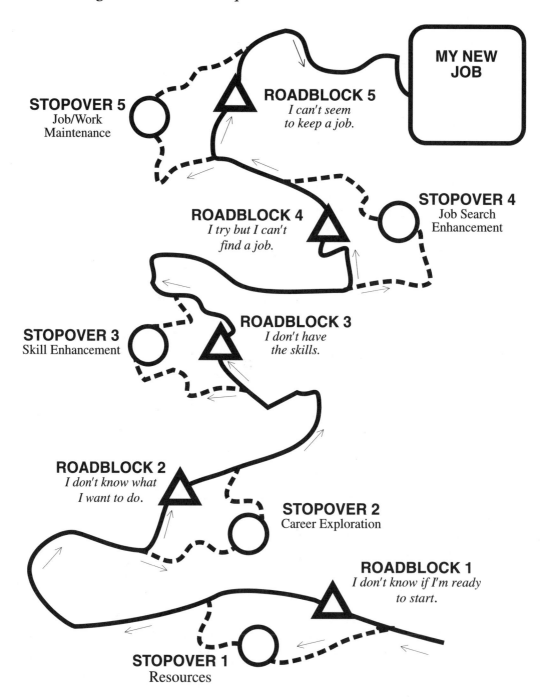

must precede any consideration of the problem. Counsellors might want to use a statement such as the following to begin this discussion:

> *"I see that you have been directed to come here for counselling. I wonder if we could begin by considering your thoughts and feelings about this?"*

As I stated in the previous chapter, the point here is to leave some space for venting of reactions to this order for mandatory participation. In this situation counsellors are essentially listening to what is being said in an understanding and non-judgmental fashion. After a period of time, I have found it helpful to ask clients if there are any issues that they would like to explore given the fact that we have to spend this time together. This then forms the basis for the initial problem identification. In situations where a problem cannot be identified, it might be appropriate to bring closure to the interview. It is interesting to note that in most circumstances, clients will choose to continue with counselling if they are provided with the initial venting period.

Clarifying the Counselling Problem

Clients who come for counselling are usually seeing a counsellor because they are in some ways "stuck." They are looking for a new perspective (reframing) for the problem they are facing. Counsellors are viewed as "reframing agents," people who can help them overcome the roadblocks they are facing. Prior to engaging in this reframing process, however, it is important that you acquire the full story of what has happened. That is, you need to understand the various facets of the problem up to the point where clients are seeking reframing, i.e. action steps that have been taken, the initial framing of the problem, the triggers for decision making, some of the determining contexts, and any external influences which have played a role. The interactive career decision making model (Figure Three) illustrates the relationship between these various components.

Clients come for counselling because they are in some ways "stuck"... looking for a new perspective. Counsellors are viewed as 'reframing agents', who can help them overcome roadblocks

Acquiring a full understanding of the story requires a careful elaboration of all aspects of the situation (cognitive, affective, behavioural, and contextual). Taking clients back over the story in greater detail is an important element in the career counselling process. A good place to begin this exploration is by looking at the **decision trigger(s)** that serves as a beginning point. Decision triggers can be either external or internal. Examples of external triggers include events such as job loss, graduation from an educational or training program, a change in marital status, death in a family, and so on. Internal triggers, on the other hand, are events such as turning a certain age (30, 40, 50, 65 years) or not achieving the goals one set earlier in life (Schlossberg & Robinson, 1996). Understanding the dynamics of the career triggers requires the use of questions such as the following:

Figure Three: Interactive Decision Making Model

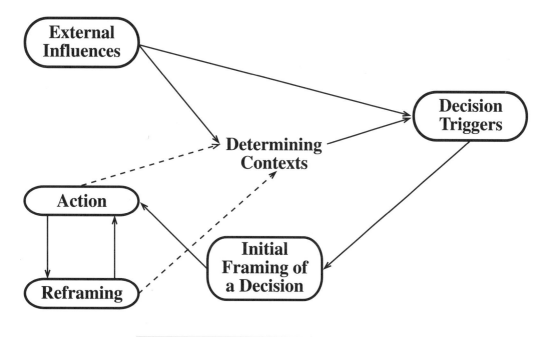

1. **First Impressions:** "*When did you first hear that (you were going to lose your job)?*" or "*When did you first feel that (you needed to make a career change)? How were you feeling when that happened?*"

2. **Transition Period:** "*What happened between the time you first heard (thought) about it and you actually left your job? What were you thinking and feeling during this time?*"

3. **Significant Others:** "*What were the reactions (actions, thoughts, feelings) of others to what was happening?*"

The main point here is to understand the story and its beginnings. Communications skills such as open ended questioning, paraphrasing, clarifying, empathy and summarizing are particularly important during this phase.

The description of the decision triggers usually includes mention of any external influences that might have contributed to the problem. An external influence is an environmental situation that leads to a particular decision trigger. For example, trade agreements between countries, stock market changes, labour market shifts, and so on can play an important role in the lives of ordinary working people. These influences are often global in nature and are difficult to control. Nevertheless, they can and do have a significant impact on career planning.

Other factors which are often mentioned during the discussion of decision triggers relate to the determining context variable. Under this heading, we find influences such as culture, the family, gender, interpersonal roles, traumatic experiences, and the basic self structure. It should be noted here that any discussion of determining contexts at this point is preliminary and will be expanded upon at a later point in the counselling process (after a full exploration of the story).

Following the discussion of triggers, the focus shifts to the **initial framing** of the problem and the **actions** that were taken. This movement from the past to the present allows for a more in-depth exploration of how the problem was initially viewed and the actions that were attempted to solve the problem (with accompanying emotions). Questions such as the following are appropriate during this phase:

> *"Let's now look at what has happened since leaving your job (deciding to make a career shift). What thoughts and feelings have you had during this period? What actions have you taken? How has what you are going through affected other people? What types of emotional and /or financial support have you received during this time period?"*

At this point it is important to remind clients of their successes (what they have learned), as well as their disappointments. It is also necessary to highlight the ways in which they have demonstrated self-directed behaviour. One of the most obvious steps which is often overlooked is the very fact that they have come for counselling. If coming to counselling is a voluntary act, it is something that they have initiated and is an indication that they are motivated to find solutions.

As clients define the problem, it is important that you not lose sight of the emotional elements embedded within the unfolding story. It is easy to get so caught up in the details that you miss this very important dimension. To help clients focus on the emotional elements associated with unemployment, I have found it helpful to have them compare their emotions to the emotional roller coaster that is illustrated in Figure Four.

Figure Four: The Roller Coaster of Unemployment

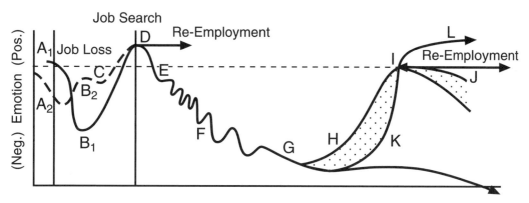

A₁. Initial negative reactions to job loss (shock, anger)

B₁. Reflection upon job loss (worry, anxiety)

A₂. Acceptance of job loss (anxiety, apprehension, denial)

B₂. Initial reaction to job loss (relief)

C. Acceptance of job loss (determined, in-control)

D. Acceptance of job loss (hopeful, optimistic, proud)

E. Initial reactions to stress associated with job search (pressure, discouragement, fear, anger, desperation)

F. Insulation from job-search-related stress (apathy)

G. Internalization of rejection (worthless, isolated, lonely, drifting)

H. Support/re-training (hopeful, understood, encouraged)

I. Maintenance of job search

J. Slippage to stress-related reactions

K. Re-assessment of self, values

L. Levelling (positive, changed)

The roller coaster diagram is based on some earlier research on the dynamics of unemployment (Borgen & Amundson, 1987). Using the diagram as a reference point helps people to normalize some of the emotional reactions they might be experiencing.

Another common problem is getting the exact sequence of events as clients tell their story. One of the counselling tools that I frequently use to help me attain this understanding is the lifeline. The lifeline looks much like a stock market index (ups and downs recorded over a period of time). An example of a lifeline is provided in Figure Five.

Figure Five: Lifeline

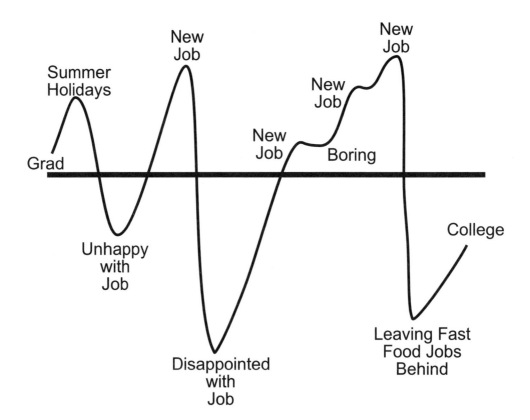

Having clients describe their story using this method helps to define the critical incidents in the story. Often a lifeline can be used as a summary after clients have described their situation. By working with clients to create this diagram, you have the opportunity to check both their understanding of events and their understanding of the relative emotional impact of each situation.

At this point the story has been clearly told, and there is a shift to another level of understanding, the **determining contexts**. As I mentioned earlier, determining contexts refer to the influences of culture, family, gender roles, other interpersonal roles, traumatic experiences, and the structure of the self (values, personality, self esteem, interests). The impact of determining influences on decision making can be illustrated with the following case description. A young man was raised in a family where the father tried to start a business but was unsuccessful and, as a result, faced bankruptcy. The influence of this event on the family and the young man was considerable; and, as the young man made his career decisions, he was careful to pick a profession where security seemed to be assured. Choosing the teaching field seemed like a logical choice and life turned out well for a period of time. With the changing economic situation, however, cutbacks in the schools were inevitable; and he found himself traumatized by the thought of losing his job. Added to this problem was the growing realization that he really didn't enjoy the teaching profession. Counselling someone under these circumstances would be impossible without having some understanding of the earlier determining influences. Understanding the earlier traumatic family events does not explain everything, but it does point to some of the factors that impede risk taking.

Exploring determining contexts is something that is not handled through the use of a few questions or exercises; it is far more complex. The starting point is listening for some of the cues during rapport building and problem defining. Clients will often make reference to situations during their description of career/life problems, and it can be helpful to focus the additional enquiry in these specific areas. It may be advisable to simply ask the person to identify some of the factors that they perceive to be influential in their career decision making. Sometimes the direct approach will cut right to the heart of the matter and help focus on the major issues. If there is sufficient time and interest, it is possible to conduct a more in-depth enquiry using a comprehensive structured interviewing approach. Whatever method is utilized, it is helpful to consider that the initial framing of problems may be heavily influenced by some earlier experiences.

Another aspect of determining influences is the self-structure which functions as a moderator with respect to the other more external influences. One example of this is the level of agency or self efficacy which a person brings to bear on a situation. "Persons with high levels of self awareness and personal agency are in a better position to respond proactively to external circumstances and exert more control over long term effects" (Amundson, 1995a, p. 12). Other aspects of the self–including values, interests, personality and aptitudes–also play a key role in shaping the experience of decision triggers and the framing and action steps which follow. In some respects the old adage "seeing is believing" needs to be replaced by the new maxim "believing is seeing." Our perspective on the world determines what we will see.

Defining the Problem
Using Metaphors

The discussion thus far has focused primarily on defining the problem through careful exploration and a consideration of events, emotions and contextual variables. For many people, metaphoric imagery is a useful means to capture the essence of their situation. Lakoff and Johnson (1980) would go so far as to suggest that "our ordinary conceptual system, in terms of which we both think and act, is fundamentally metaphorical in nature" (p.3). Metaphors are the ways in which we understand and experience events in terms of their connection to other events. For example, we might feel elated and suggest that we are "flying high." Metaphors help us to visualize situations; and by using relatively simple visual images, we are in a better position to posit actions.

Metaphors help us to visualize situations; and by using relatively simple visual images, we are in a better position to posit actions.

Helping clients to be aware of their current metaphors and to develop new images becomes a major career counselling task.

Metaphors are also closely connected to flexibility and creativity. According to Combs and Freedman (1990):

> "Any single metaphor is a particular version of a particular part of the world. When people have only one metaphor for a situation, their creativity is limited. The more metaphors they have to choose from for a given situation, the more choice and flexibility they have in how to handle it. Finding multiple metaphors expands the realm of creativity." (p. 32)

For many clients, the changing labour market has required a shift toward greater flexibility and creativity as they attempt to cope with changing realities (Herr, 1993). Helping clients to be aware of their current metaphors and to develop new images becomes a major career counselling task.

As clients tell their stories, they will often use metaphoric images in their descriptions. Listening for these images is an important counselling skill. Embedded within the images is information about how they see problems and how they see their abilities to overcome the barriers they are facing. For example, one unemployed client described her situation as one in which she felt that she was sitting at one end of a table and being ignored by the kitchen staff. Some people were getting ample amounts of food while others sat at the side and waited for any crumbs that might be dropped. In this instance government and big business were the people dishing out the food. She was clearly sitting with the "have-nots" and felt that there was no way to get what she wanted. This metaphor is interesting in that the client was viewing her situation from an essentially passive stance. She felt hopeless about possibilities and waited passively for something to happen. Using this metaphor as a picture of the problem, I was able to suggest changes to the metaphor that enhanced greater personal agency and action. The client learned some assertive behaviours and began exploring other ways of getting the food (entrepreneurship). The metaphor was a good vehicle for stating the problem and exploring possible solutions.

As part of my supervisory activities (discussed more in Chapter Eight), I have encouraged counsellors to take a more active role by creating metaphors for clients based on their observations. These metaphors can serve as a summary, one in which the counsellor is trying to express his/her understanding of the problem. To illustrate this process, consider the drawing in Figure Six which defines the problem from the perspective of one counsellor.

Figure Six: Case Drawing

This drawing was put together towards the end of the first session and captures some of the essential elements of the story. The client in this drawing is standing under a cloud with a barrage of problems (raindrops) coming down upon her. She has a difficult relationship with her parents, her room in the basement is damp and unbearable, she has little money, her grades at school are suffering, and her boyfriend has left her. The client sees some sunshine off in the distance but isn't sure how to get there. Within this drawing, there is a clear indication of the difficulties and the desire to move to another place. At this point, few ideas have been generated about how to get out from under the rain cloud or at least how to acquire an umbrella.

The metaphor is a good way to take the problem out from the person (externalization) and move it to another level. In this externalized form, it is possible to consider various ways of changing the metaphor. Using the examples that have been described thus far, one can see ways of altering metaphors to increase the sense of optimism, personal agency and direction. It is often easier to consider solutions when the problem has been moved to a more external position.

Analyzing a Case

I would like to illustrate this section on problem definition by analyzing an actual case situation using the concepts of metaphoric imagery and the interactive decision making model. The career story I have chosen comes from the writings of the poet Carl Leggo who muses in poetic form (Roads to Nineveh) about the career path he has chosen. The choice of a poet for this analysis is deliberate in that it reinforces the notions of imagination and creativity and shows that the concepts of interactive decision making have wide application.

ROADS TO NINEVEH

Corner Brook 1970, 1988

My high school principal said,
You ought to be a teacher.
I said, No way. Almost two
decades faded away. I
circled back to my old school.
The principal was retired, long
gone. I was a teacher. Surprised

St. John's 1970-1976

I never wanted to be a teacher.
I wanted to be an astronomer
and watch the heavens, or
even a poet and write the heavens.
I took a vocational interests inventory.
I learned I ought to be a farrier,
even though I am scared of horses.

Robert's Arm 1976-1978

Broke, I slipped into teaching.
My first year I taught grade seven
with forty-eight students.
I woke up in an alien world,
a small place where everybody
knew God's mind on everything.
I tried to fit in. I didn't fit. I left.

Toronto 1978-1979

for the big city, a world alone.
I planned to be a pastor, but
after two months of seminary
like a cemetery, the call passed, now
sure a pastor had to be pasteurized
when I wanted to be impure, rough,
germy, germinating. So, I left

Stephenville 1979-1984

for a little school in a town
on the ocean, a small farm
perhaps, an avocation and a vocation,
        where I was determined to fit,
but taught with fire in my eyes
and heart till the school committee
called me dangerous. I was. I left

Fredericton 1984-1986

and left

Edmonton 1986-1988

and left

Corner Brook 1988-1989

and left

Vancouver 1989-present

When UBC invited me,
I presented myself a poet
who did not fit, no line,
and found a home for poets
where I was not even looking,
and now I teach teachers, ask
them their sense of vocation.

Like Jonah who called to Nineveh,
rejected the call, tried to reject the call,
ran in the opposite direction,
but ended up in Nineveh anyway,
no escape, trapped in a big fish belly,
vomited on the shore of Nineveh,
still reluctant, sulks for days,

I do not know in the sentence
the locution or location of my vocation.
Where is the call coming from?
Who is calling me?
I have no vocation, a noun;
I have a vocating, a verb.
At least I am not vacating.

I am not responding to a vocation.
I am a vocation, a verb of vocation,
always continuous, present, now.
Jonah was not running away;
Jonah was running his vocation.
As I have and do. All the strange
twists are part of my verbal role.

I have not been called to teaching.
I am a teacher, teaching always. No
vacation from vocation, no avocation,
my call is all. I live my teaching;
my teaching is lived. I have turned
a circle, round and round, to know
I am a teacher, a farrier even,

who shoes students in order
to shoo them away, no
reluctance to walk with them,
only wanting them to hear
the poetry in their journeys.
I am a teacher, I am a farrier
who shoes and shoos students.

The career story that has been outlined in the poem contains within
it some interesting images and dynamics. The author struggles with the
image of career as something chosen or a form of destiny. The idea of a
"calling" flows through the poem. The image of Jonah's call to Nineveh
serves to highlight an ever-present presence. The high school principal
also plays a key role in foretelling, suggesting in the early years that
teaching was the call. True to form, some years later Carl finds himself,
despite all his efforts to avoid the call, teaching in his old school. The

irony of the situation suggests a Greek tragedy, but there is always another chapter, the most recent being that of a poet. The role of teacher transforms itself from noun to verb and teaching becomes a life work.

Other subplots within this career story include his foray into the ministry where he finds that to be a minister one needs to be pasteurized. Seeking a more vigorous life, he returns to teaching. There are also attempts to focus on farming and the country life as an avocation within a vocation. Again, success is not to be found.

Contained within the story are also elements of entrapment where Carl does battle with the parochial school system. At some level he wants to fit in and live the good life but finds himself unable to make the necessary sacrifices. He struggles and yearns for a different life. Under unbearable conditions, he often retreats to various educational programs as a way out. Throughout all of these struggles, there are elements of falsehood to self. Finally as the interview at UBC looms before him, he chooses to cast aside the old identity and face the world wearing the garments of the poet. It is through this new self-structure that the poet now creates a new career direction.

In many ways the story that Carl has woven for us is a modern legend. The foretelling of the principal casts a spell (a calling) and sets the scene for the ensuing struggle. Following this opening, there is struggle and despair as the author is continuously ensnared by the calling despite his efforts to break free. After numerous failed attempts, there is the realization that the truth lies within the acceptance of a new identity. At this point the spell is broken and Carl creates a new identity in a new place. But, unlike fables of old, the story continues and Carl must find the means to sustain himself as a poet in an educational environment. This is the challenge that lies ahead.

As a counsellor working at the metaphoric level, I would seek to make Carl aware of these dynamics and also to help him craft the next chapter of the tale. What would be particularly important here is that Carl maintain the sense of identity and personal agency that characterized his breakthrough experience. Educational systems, even at the university level, have ways of entrapping the unwary. Finding and keeping the freedom of the poetic existence requires ongoing vigilance and proactivity. Using the employability dimensions that were mentioned earlier, Carl will need to continue to work at job maintenance skills.

Placing a story such as this within the confines of the interactive decision making model seems at first glance to be somewhat incongruous. There is little doubt that the story flows very nicely into a steady stream of metaphoric imagery. And yet, there are elements which point to determining contexts, decision triggers, initial framing, actions, and reframing. Certainly the end result is a transformation experience which places teaching within an acceptable realm, a form of reframing. Prior to this, there are many instances of framing and action taking which resulted in frustration and despair. It could be argued that many of the difficulties with "teaching" might be the result of finding employment within a restrictive educational system which was at odds with Carl's basic values and personality (determining contexts). The triggers for finding a job as a teacher seem to have been pragmatic, tied to financial needs and the desire to provide for a growing family.

As one looks at this particular career path over a period of time, it is evident that there is a certain negative and recurring cycle to events. Carl struggles to break free at various points through seeking further education (a common action strategy for many people seeking an escape from unsatisfactory work experiences) and these moments are positive and fleeting. The circle remains unbroken and he continues to find himself in unsatisfactory teaching situations with few apparent options. In this respect he is like many clients who find themselves stuck within cycles of negativity. Under such conditions, it is easy to imagine that one is a pawn in the system with little opportunity to find escape. And yet, Carl did find a way out by casting aside the falseness of his earlier image and by seeing himself as a poet seeking to help people to live poetically. Through self examination, he struck a note for personal efficacy and a new vision (identity) was born. It is the facilitation of this process of self examination which often falls to the career counsellor. As was mentioned earlier, it also falls to the counsellor to help the client discover the challenges that might lie ahead, in this case the self management of career. The transforming or reframing experience creates a new context, but awareness and ongoing vigilance is necessary to protect against a re-occurrence of the earlier entrapment. Carl's metaphoric imagery is a useful foundation for developing self understanding and also creating an awareness of potential new challenges.

Summary

The process of defining the client problem often serves a dual function in that while the problem is being clarified, new solutions begin to emerge. In many instances the major problem is the fact that clients have a difficult time sorting out the various components of their problem(s). Under these circumstances the distinction between problem definition and problem resolution become blurred. Once the focus on the problem is adjusted, the pathway toward problem resolution becomes more visible and sometimes completely obvious.

In the next three chapters, I will be discussing various methods of helping clients to move further towards the resolution of their problems. In taking this step toward other methods of problem resolution, I will first be looking at systematic and dynamic self-assessment approaches (Chapters Four and Five) and then in the subsequent chapter (Chapter Six) at some practical methods of connecting, deciding and preparing. Moving into these other areas does not necessarily mean that the door can be shut with respect to problem definition. As counselling progresses, new aspects of problems can arise and in some instances the entire problem can shift into another arena. At each step of the process, you will need to be cognizant of the shifting nature of client problems. It can be helpful to identify those moments when there is some change to the problems that have been identified. In this respect, the movement forwards is never completely sequential. There is usually some back and forth movement and periodically, even a dramatic shift in emphasis. This is particularly the case with career counselling since many clients use this form of counselling emphasis to mask more personal concerns.

Of course, not all situations lend themselves to seeking resolution of client issues. In many instances, the next step is toward some type of action plan which involves other counselling agencies. Under these circumstances you will need to assume a referral role and help point clients toward the appropriate services. The roadmap that was described earlier is a good way to conceptualize problems and also to show clients how they can address barriers by using various stopovers (counselling and educational programs) to overcome their difficulties. Chapter Seven addresses in greater detail some of the issues associated with termination and client referral.

As counselling progresses, new aspects of problems can arise and in some instances the entire problem can shift into another arena. At each step of the process, you will need to be cognizant of the shifting nature of client problems.

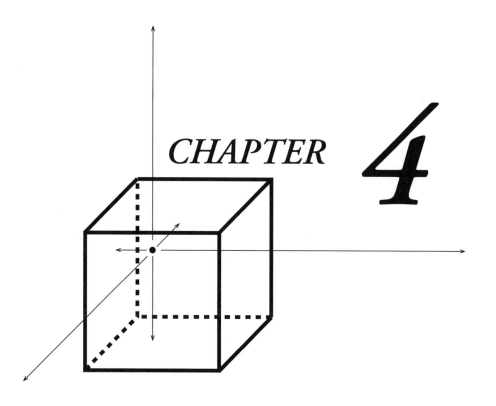

CHAPTER 4

PROBLEM RESOLVING TASKS:

Systematic Self-Assessment

As was mentioned in the previous chapter, a certain amount of "fuzziness" exists between problem defining tasks and problem resolving tasks. Thus, as we move forward you may find that some of the strategies that are presented here could have some application to more clearly defining the problem. Rather than viewing this overlap as a problem, I see it as a reflection of the holistic nature of counselling. The real world is never as clearly differentiated as our theories might suggest.

This chapter and the next one focus on self-assessment tasks. In some instances these tasks help clients rediscover ideas they once held, but which were "lost" due to life circumstances. This is particularly the case with self perceptions that may be diminished because of external pressures. In other situations entirely new connections may be necessary in order to cope with the problems that have emerged. Whatever the case, the emphasis here is upon changing the way in which people think and feel about themselves and the problems they are facing.

A distinguishing feature of the self-assessment tasks included in this chapter is the fact that they are relatively straight forward and contain a set procedure for exploration; in other words, they are more systematic. I recognize in making this distinction that it is somewhat arbitrary. In many respects it is merely a matter of degree rather than kind.

Whatever the case, the emphasis here is upon changing the way in which people think and feel about themselves and the problems they are facing.

The tasks described in the next chapter also contain some systematic elements. Once again there is a certain fuzziness in making this separation, but as was stated above this is simply a reflection of the world in which we live.

Exploring Through Information

A. The Internet

The internet provides an excellent resource for occupational information, but it is more than just a repository for facts and figures. It also can be used to facilitate a broadly-based career exploration search. A variety of exercises and information is available through a number of general web sites. A few sites available at the time of writing are:

- The Riley Guide: Employment Opportunities and Job Resources on the Internet
  (http://www.dbm.com/jobguide)

- Work Search: The Counsellor Resource Centre
  (http://worksearch.gc.ca/crc)

- WorkWeb: Canada's Online Campus Career Centre
  (http://www.cacee.com/mainf398.html#null)

- What Color is Your Parachute: Job Hunting Online
  (http://www.washingtonpost.com/parachute)

Other sites which list specific occupational information will be described in the next chapter in the section on gathering necessary labour market information.

Keeping up with the internet is, of course, a very challenging task given the continuous generation of new sites and exposure to vast quantities of new information. As clients engage in exploration through various internet sites, they will need to debrief their experiences with trained career counsellors. While the sites are often designed to be relatively complete in and of themselves, in most instances there is a need for some discussion with another person to consolidate the learning.

If you are planning to involve clients with activities on the internet, it can be helpful to consider some of the criteria for information usage as suggested by Wurman (1989). The first step would be to be sure that the clients are, in fact, interested and willing to consider the new information which they are gathering. The information must also be organized into a structure or framework that is understandable to them. Achieving this goal often depends on the way the new information is related to other existing ideas. It is sometimes worthwhile to have clients work with the information and test the validity of what is being proposed. Meeting the information goals that Wurman has defined requires ongoing involvement in the career counselling process. Years ago, when computers were first being introduced into career counselling, there was concern that the need for counsellors would be reduced. It soon became evident that while many clients appreciated the opportunity to work on a computer, there was a significant need for debriefing after the experience. There is no reason to think that the situation will reverse itself no matter what advances are made in computer technology. In the final analysis, people want and need the opportunity to discuss their situation with another human being.

A recent article by Sampson, Lolodinsky and Greens (1997) provides a good summary of some of the possibilities and problems associated with the use of the internet. While the internet offers some exciting opportunities in terms of information access, it also can be misused by inadequately trained or overworked counsellors.

B. Self-Help Books

The thriving self-0help book market is a good illustration of people's thirst for psychological knowledge. Sorting through the various pieces of information, however, can be challenging and this is an area where you can offer your clients some practical assistance. There are many situations where you might find it worthwhile to recommend particular books or articles to address specific topics of concern. These readings can be used as a basis for discussion within future counselling sessions.

C. Psychoeducational Instruction

In addition to directing people to specific self-help books, I have also at times incorporated some direct instruction into counselling sessions. This instruction can focus on many different topics. For example, I have found myself going back to some basic "transactional analysis" principles to illustrate points about motivation, interpersonal relationships, repeating patterns of behaviour and so on. In one case, a woman was trying to upgrade her skills so that she could return to work. Her children were grown up and working outside the home, and her husband was making a good wage at his job. Despite the apparent "rightness" of the situation, she found herself struggling with the decision that she had made. In reviewing some of the family dynamics, I found it helpful to illustrate some family patterns using transactional analysis principles (Berne, 1964). This educational "moment" was helpful throughout the counselling process as she reflected upon other interpersonal interactions. She found herself repeatedly falling into the "Nurturing Parent" role and realized that at times her rescuing behaviours led her into interactions which interfered with the change in career direction that she was attempting.

Questioning Strategies Which Emphasize Possibilities

In recent years there has been a growing trend toward the use of strategies which are more future focused and which emphasize possibilities rather than problems, i.e. narrative and brief/solution-focused counselling (De Shazer, 1985; O'Hanlon & Weiner-Davis; 1989; White & Epston, 1990; and Friedman, 1993). From this perspective, it is important initially to listen to problems but to maintain the emphasis on finding ways to resolve difficulties. One aspect of this approach is the use of particular questioning strategies which serve to identify strengths, emphasize positive changes and suggest possible solutions. Listed below are five examples of different questioning strategies:

1. Description of between session changes

Questions in this realm focus on changes that are made between sessions. The assumption is made that positive things are happening and need to be reported in counselling sessions. In using this type of question, you need to frame the enquiry within a context of positive expectations. For example, you would ask clients to *"describe some of the positive changes they have noticed during the week"* rather than asking if anything positive has happened during this time period. The first question makes the assumption that something good has happened.

Working in a collaborative fashion, you can ask clients to pay particular attention to how their problems are diminishing between sessions.

As a support for this approach, "homework" activities can be assigned which focus on some of the positive changes that are happening. Working in a collaborative fashion, you can ask clients to pay particular attention to how their problems are diminishing between sessions. For example, they may feel anxious when making calls to employers. As counselling progresses, there is an expectation that this anxiety will diminish; and a careful monitoring of the change helps to reinforce the positive gains that are being made.

2. Coping strategies in other situations

Clients facing problems often become so focused on the problems that they forget that this is not the first time that they have faced problems. In other areas of their lives they are coping or have successfully coped with problems, and these strengths need to be emphasized. I have noticed, for example, when working with refugees, that they often do not have the same level of anxiety over unemployment as some others in the mainstream culture. As they reflect upon this matter, they often comment that after facing bombs and refugee camps, unemployment is really a rather minor challenge. Just to have survived is a remarkable accomplishment, and they feel confident in their abilities to handle the challenges of unemployment. While many people do not have such dramatic stories to tell, they do have a broader range of experiences to draw upon. Helping them to put their problems into perspective can be a useful way to have them realize that they have considerable internal and external resources to draw upon.

> *In other areas of their lives they are coping or have successfully coped with problems, and these strengths need to be emphasized.*

Clients facing problems often are confused and disoriented about what to do next. As they think about other problems they have faced, they can also begin to identify the steps which brought about problem resolution. Some of the strategies which were successful for them in other situations may have application in their current dilemma.

When using this approach, you need to help clients pinpoint situations where successful coping was utilized and to further analyze these events to specify the specific strategies that were effective.

3. Exception finding questions

The focus on client problems can often be so all-consuming that it appears that everything is negative. Rather than accepting this bleak scenario, you can search for moments where the problem is not so imposing. For example, a client reported that whenever he went into an interview situation, he "froze" and found that he became stiff and stilted in his response to questions. The client could provide any number of examples of this type of self-defeating behaviour. After listening to several examples of the problem, I asked him to shift his focus to the times in interviewing when he felt more relaxed. While there were many negative examples, there were also some times when the he was not "frozen." Helping him to articulate the positive examples provided a foundation upon which further positive changes could be built.

> *Helping clients to realize that their problem situations are not uniformly negative is an important insight. It is within the "positive cracks" (exceptions) that strengths can be recognized.*

Exception finding can also be expanded to homework activities where clients are asked to work collaboratively between sessions to report examples of situations where problems were not evident. Helping clients to realize that their problem situations are not uniformly negative is an important insight. It is within the "positive cracks" (exceptions) that strengths can be recognized.

The identification of exceptions is not something that rests solely with clients. You can also bring your observations to the discussion, particularly when you have noticed contradictions between beliefs and observed behaviours. Challenging clients with their strengths can serve as an important impetus for change (Borgen & Amundson, 1996). Counsellor statements such as the following are reflective of this form of strength challenge:

> "*In our earlier conversation, you indicated that you weren't able to think quickly on your feet during interviews. I've noticed, however, in the recent activity that you were quite adept at changing the focus when you saw that what you were doing wasn't working. It would seem to me that this would be a good illustration of thinking on your feet.*"

When making these type of strength challenge observations, it is important to use behavioural description as the basis for challenge. If the comments are too general, clients will feel good about what is being said but discount the believability of the observations. You can probably think of many people who pour out the positive comments but have little impact because they are not specific with their observations.

4. Scaling Questions

Many clients when looking at their problems see where they want to get to, but have few ideas about how to get there. Using a metaphor, they see themselves at the bottom of a mountain and they want to get to the top; but they find themselves going back and forth in their minds with few steps in-between. Sometimes it can be helpful to have them think of problem solving as a journey with various rest stops and challenges along the way. Scaling helps clients identify their most desired outcomes, what they believe they can reasonably hope to achieve in their present situation, and what would be some examples of downward motion. The scaling system that was described in Chapter Two (Mutually Determining Counselling

Scaling helps clients identify their most desired outcomes, what they believe they can reasonably hope to achieve in their present situation, and what would be some examples of downward motion.

Goals) is a good illustration of this process, i.e. +2 the ideal; +1 a reasonable goal; 0 the current situation; -1 a negative turn; -2 an absolute disaster.

Scaling can also be used to look at how clients are feeling on a ten point scale. You can look at how they are feeling at the present moment, where they would have rated themselves last week, how they see things improving in the time ahead, and so on. I have found that it is helpful when asking for these evaluations to have clients use movement to illustrate the various positions. For example, I will suggest that one wall in the room represents a plus ten and the other wall a zero. Clients are then requested to walk to the place where they are at the present moment and then are encouraged to change positions to reflect specific times in the past and what they are hoping for in the future.

The advantage of scaling is that it helps to define goals and emotions in concrete terms. Clients can look at their current position and then see how they have changed and reflect on the changes that might lie ahead. In this respect it is really a form of externalization that takes internal problems and makes them more visible and, thus, easier to address in a more direct fashion.

5. Miracle Questions

When people are problem solving, they usually look at the past, where they are today and what they are hoping to achieve in the future. With this linear-time perspective, problem solving is usually conducted in a straightforward fashion.

Sometimes it can be helpful to change perspectives by having clients imagine (visualize) that they have reached the goal(s) they have set for themselves. Rather than asking clients to look ahead to the goals they hope to reach, ask them to imagine that they have achieved their objectives (a miracle has happened). In formulating this goal, ask them to describe all the specific elements of their achievement. Help them to establish themselves firmly within the position that they were hoping to achieve. From the point of goal attainment, they then look back at what had to happen in order for this to occur. Shifting from a forward-looking perspective to one in which they are looking backwards can lead to new insights and a greater appreciation for the steps that lie between where they are now and where they would like to be. As with the previous scaling questions, it can be helpful to have clients act this out in the counselling room, i.e. standing at one side of the room and walking over to the other side and then looking backwards. The physical movement adds another dimension to counselling and helps people to focus on the task at hand.

When clients are in a position of having realized their goals (visually), they often recognize that a lot more might be required than they originally thought. At this point you need to help them think through all of the steps and assess whether they are willing to make the commitment. Often clients set unrealistic goals and this exercise can help them recognize what is actually involved. In some instances it is better to set smaller goals which are more realistic given the circumstances.

> *Shifting from a forward-looking perspective to one in which they are looking backwards can lead to new insights and a greater appreciation for the steps that lie between where they are now and where they would like to be.*

Another variation on this exercise is to increase flexibility by asking clients how many different pathways there might be to the goals that they have set for themselves. By approaching the task in this way, clients have the opportunity to see that there may be more than one pathway that they could follow. Challenging clients to think more broadly helps prepare them for unexpected barriers that might emerge along the way.

Comprehensive Career Exploration: The Career Pathways Program

Many people find themselves in the career stream without having access to any type of comprehensive career exploration. They haven't taken the time nor had the opportunity to understand themselves and to explore their world as well as the changing labour market. While working with unemployed clients, I have had the opportunity to see some of the positive benefits of taking some time away from working life. Most people would not choose to repeat their unemployment experience, but they have commented on the positive effects of conducting a comprehensive personal and labour market career exploration.

> *Most people have commented on the positive effects of conducting a comprehensive personal and labour market career exploration.*

One of the tools that has been helpful for clients in addressing this issue has been the use of the Wheel that was presented earlier (Figure One). With this model there is the recognition that career goal setting requires information from a number of different internal and external domains. The career exploration workbook *Career Pathways* adopts this systematic approach and provides a set of qualitative assessment activities to cover each segment of the Wheel (Amundson & Poehnell, 1996). Thus, there are activities to cover interests, values, skills and personal style in the personal domain and, at a more external level, activities which focus on the perceptions of significant others, educational background, work and leisure experiences, and the labour market. Figure Seven illustrates how a segment of the Wheel might look once it is completed—in this case the personal style piece of the Wheel is presented:

Figure Seven: A Wheel Segment

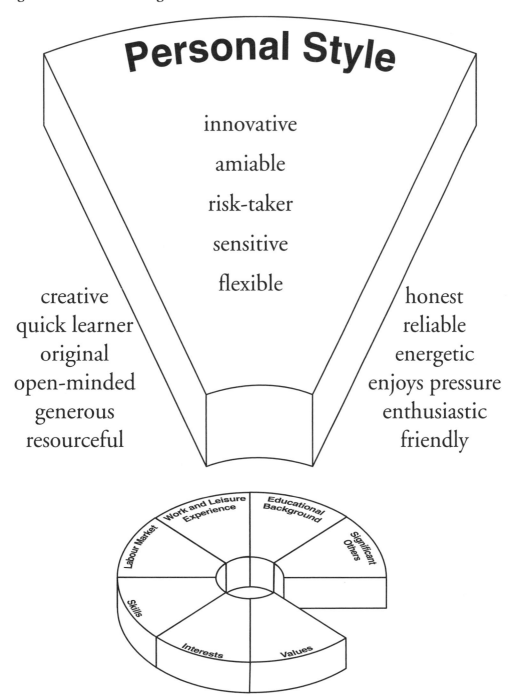

Personal Style

innovative

amiable

risk-taker

sensitive

flexible

creative
quick learner
original
open-minded
generous
resourceful

honest
reliable
energetic
enjoys pressure
enthusiastic
friendly

Labour Market

Work and Leisure Experience

Educational Background

Significant Others

Skills

Interests

Values

The client, in this example, has identified a number of important personality traits. The most important characteristics are placed in the centre of the diagram and the others on the side. The visual presentation of each segment of the Wheel forms an impressive visual image when it is all put together as a total picture.

According to Goldman (1992), there are certain advantages to using qualitative assessment methods such as those used within the Career Pathways program:

> (a) qualitative assessment usually is more informal and allows for more flexibility on the part of the counselor in its use, as compared with standardized tests; (b) qualitative methods involve the client more actively in the search for self-awareness and can more readily lead directly and immediately into counseling interactions, and (c) qualitative methods, because they are usually not restricted to pre-set scales and scoring categories, tend to be more open-ended, divergent, and holistic in their interpretation and discussion. (p. 616)

While I agree with much of the argument being put forward by Goldman, I can also see how some additional standardized assessment measures could still be helpful, particularly with respect to skill assessment (aptitudes).

Participants working through the Career Pathways program have the option of completing all or some of the qualitative assessment activities covered in the workbook. They also can supplement particular exercises by using additional qualitative techniques or standardized assessment measures. Some common additions include the Self Directed Search (Holland, 1985b), the Myers-Briggs Type Indicator (Myers & McCaulley, 1985), the Individual Style Survey (Amundson, 1989b) and the GATB (U.S. Dept. of Labour, 1979).

As you consider each of the segments of the Wheel, it is important to recognize the uniqueness of each person. For one person, personal values may be of paramount importance, while for someone else it might be the input from significant others. To capture the uniqueness of the individual, you may find it helpful to have clients construct their own personal Wheel using a blank form (the size of each segment to be determined by the individual). Another visual aid is to have people transfer their results to a large Wheel on a flip chart or cut out each of the "pieces of the pie" and arrange them in a circular fashion on a large sheet of paper.

A shorter version of the Career Pathways program (*Career Pathways: Quick Trip*) has recently been developed (Amundson & Poehnell, 1998). This adapted program focuses on a few key elements from the original program and makes good use of the personal career exploration Wheel.

There are several other broadly-based career exploration programs. Redekopp, Day, Magnusson, and Durnford (1993), for example, utilize an in-depth interviewing procedure to help clients develop career self-portraits. Super, Osborne, Walsh, Brown and Niles (1992) use what they call the Career-Development Assessment and Counselling model (C-DAC). This approach has a strong developmental component and relies on several standardized test batteries. With all of these systems there is a focus on comprehensive and systematic career exploration.

The Pattern Identification Exercise

The model of career exploration that has just been described (Career Pathways) starts with an overarching view, the Wheel, and then focuses on specific activities. Another way to approach career exploration is to start with specific incidents and then move toward the larger picture. To facilitate this movement, I have found it helpful to start with a detailed description and then to use a guided inquiry procedure to facilitate the analysis and ultimately the application. The development of this latter approach is based on the work of Young, Becker & Pike (1970) in the field of rhetoric. They developed a system of questioning based on changing perspectives and used this approach to understand novel situations.

A careful examination of experience will reveal significant life patterns. These patterns are unique and are embedded within the lived experience of each person.

The pattern identification exercise is based on the assumption that a careful examination of experience will reveal significant life patterns. These patterns are unique and are embedded within the lived experience of each person. To illustrate, consider how people involve themselves in a sport such as tennis. Several people may indicate an interest in the sport, but it is only when you examine the particular experiences that you see the differences. For one person, playing tennis may be a social activity, one in which they have the opportunity to be with others in a friendly and congenial atmosphere. As they describe positive and negative experiences, they will undoubtedly reflect upon some of the good times socializing both on and off the court. For another person, the experience may be very different. The competition might be the significant factor. And for someone else the physical exercise may be of paramount importance. While drawn together by the common bond of tennis, each person brings to the situation very different needs and perspectives.

Understanding these perspectives and needs can facilitate personal insights which have direct application to career choice, job search, and job satisfaction.

In using this method any number of different types of experience can be analyzed. I have found it helpful to begin with some of the domains which people are less likely to associate with traditional career exploration. Leisure experiences are often a good starting point. People are usually willing to talk quite candidly about their leisure experiences. It is an easy way to initiate a discussion and the conversation flows smoothly. Of course, not all life patterns are contained within one set of leisure experiences. For a more comprehensive analysis it can be helpful to sample experiences from a number of different domains, i.e. working life, education, spiritual experiences, family life, etc.

The steps of inquiry associated with the pattern identification exercise are listed below (Amundson, 1995b):

1. Ask the client to think about a particular activity; this activity can come from a number of different domains. Once the activity has been defined, ask the person to think about a specific time when it was very enjoyable and a time when it was less so.

2. Have the client describe in detail the positive and negative experiences. Some questions can be asked at this point to facilitate a full description of events. Ask about the people involved, feelings, thoughts, challenges, successes and motivations. What are the particular dynamics that differentiate the positive and negative dynamics? Depending on the situation, it may be helpful to extend the questioning to some of the contextual issues. Ask about how their interest developed over time and what they project for the future. As the story is told it is helpful for the counsellor to write down what it being said, either on a flip chart or a large piece of paper clearly visible to the client. This information will serve as the foundation for the analysis; and,

thus, it is important to get down on paper everything that is said. (Generally I am not in favour of note taking during a session, and it can be helpful to discuss this beforehand if it might be an issue.) Whatever is being written down should be in clear view for the client as well as the counsellor.

3. After a full discussion, have the client consider what types of patterns are suggested by the information that has been generated. Give the client every opportunity to make connections and provide ongoing support and encouragement. Ask how each specific piece of information reflects something about the client, i.e. goals, values, aptitudes, personal style, interests (from the Wheel). During this period, you can provide some input. The statements you make should be tentative and be positively linked with client comments. While this can be an excellent opportunity for reframing, it is important not to lose sight of the contribution made by the client.

4. Following the identification of themes, you move to application issues. As above, the client speaks first and then you follow with your comments. The question here is how personal information relates to career choice and action planning.

This process can be illustrated by the visual map illustrated in Figure Eight. As is clearly indicated on the visual map, there is a general movement from description, to pattern identification, to application.

To illustrate the PIE method, consider the case of a young man who was working as a car salesman but was having difficulty making sales. He seemed to like his job but wasn't having much success with it. The leisure experience that he described involved tennis. He referred to a positive incident where he was playing a good player and was "at the top of his game." His strokes were crisp, both on the forehand and the backhand. When he described the negative experience, he referred to another time when he was playing very poorly. He was overhitting the ball and having

Figure Eight: The PIE

Description

Pattern

Application

1.
Identify an activity from leisure, education, or work that is particularly enjoyable. Think about a specific time when it was very enjoyable or positive and a specific time when it was very negative.
Write this at the top of a sheet.

+   **-**

2.
Describe sequentially in detail these positive and negative experiences.
List the descriptions in parallel columns on either side below the name of the activity.

2. (cont'd)
Use questions to facilitate a full description of events, people involved, feelings, thoughts, challenges, successes, outcomes, motivations, dynamics, etc.

3.
What does this information say about you as a person?
Seek to draw out the client's goals, values, skills, personal style, interests, etc.
Look for patterns. List these points between the columns of information on the two experiences.

4.
What does this suggest regarding your career choice or career planning?
List these findings below the general characteristics.

a difficult time keeping the ball in the court. As we looked at this situation, what became apparent was the focus on technical proficiency versus actually winning a point or the game. In many ways this was similar to his experience in sales–he enjoyed meeting people and making the sales pitch but had difficulty actually closing the sale. He was so focused on getting the information out to the customer that he never got to the next step. This case brings up an interesting question, "Is it possible for him to change?" While it is extremely difficult to alter a pattern, it is not impossible. In this case the young man had to practise the final stage of salesmanship. This worked for awhile, but his heart was really in a different place and he ended up going back to school to pursue an Education degree. Even within education, however, it was important to learn how to get a commitment, to "close the sale"; and he continued striving toward that goal.

There are several advantages to using the PIE approach for career exploration. The most obvious advantage is the fact that rather than initiating separate inquiries with respect to interests, values and so on, it is possible to utilize one procedure. The inquiry that is conducted has credibility since it is based on life experiences with interpretation that is client validated. Clients through this approach are engaged in an activity which not only provides insights but also teaches a procedure for ongoing analysis. Positive reports have been obtained from a wide range of clients. Comments often refer to the surprisingly potent nature of the activity. One limitation of the PIE method is its reliance on description and analysis by clients. The effectiveness of the procedure is somewhat dependent on the cognitive abilities of both the client and the counsellor.

Task Analysis

Another activity which uses an in-depth analysis process is that of task analysis. Many clients find themselves in situations where they are studying or working in an area where they are not really satisfied. Under these circumstances, it can be helpful for them to analyze their experiences using a method of task analysis. The in-depth analysis allows them to analyze their experiences with respect to satisfaction, competency and perceived importance.

The first step in this procedure is to break the broad experience down into the component parts. Ask them to think of the tasks that are part of their everyday routine (in school or at work). For instance, suppose that one was considering the experiences associated with being in a college program. Some of the tasks that might be identified are: going to class (perhaps here you could separate different types of classes); doing specific homework assignments; studying for exams; doing class projects or papers; participating in extra-curricular activities; getting to and from classes; informal meetings with friends; and informal discussions with instructors. As you help clients identify these tasks, it is important to be as concrete as possible and to sub-divide categories where appropriate. In the example used above, the types of classes might be appropriate to specify. Some classes might be more theoretical while others might have a more experiential focus.

After identifying up to ten component tasks, there is an attempt to rank order them in terms of how much time is associated with each activity. After clients have completed the rank ordering, ask them to make a series of bar graphs rating the various activities according to the following dimensions (the graphs can be completed separately or done together for comparative purposes):

1. **Satisfaction**: How enjoyable do you find each of the tasks?

2. **Importance**: How valuable do you find each of the tasks?

3. **Competence**: To what degree do you have the necessary skills and attitudes to handle each of the tasks?

A sample of a completed assignment is included in Figure Nine.

The main advantage of task analysis is that it is visual and creates a visual image of the problem. When I use this method, there is an opportunity for the client to assess carefully the relative impact of each of the components. There are some problems which are well suited to this form of assessment. For instance, some people find that most of their time is taken up with tasks that they do not value or enjoy. Others might be struggling with the fact that they are good at what they do, but just don't find much enjoyment in the tasks. These and other problems are highlighted through creating a visual map of their work life experience. Through gaining insight, clients are in a better position to begin making changes.

---

*The main advantage
of task analysis is that it is visual,
and creates a visual image
of the problem.*

Figure Nine: Task Analysis Chart

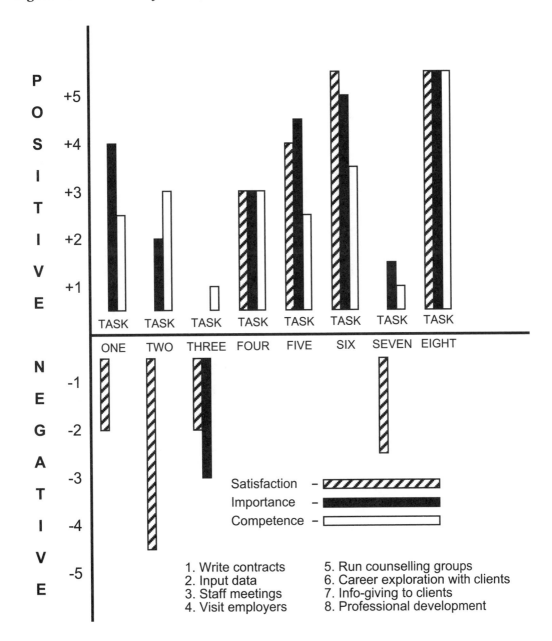

Achievement Profiling

Both the PIE activity and Task Analysis rely on a snapshot approach to exploration. That is, the major focus for the in-depth career exploration is on particular events. Another way to construe the process is through more of a developmental process where events are examined over a longer period of time.

The basic idea with achievement profiling is to have people review their achievements over an extended period of time. The time period for analysis can be as short as a few months or as long as an entire life time depending on the circumstances. As with the PIE activity, the focus is on identifying some of the recurring life patterns that are reflected in various activities of the client.

*have people review
their achievements over an
extended period of time
... as short as a few months or
as long as an entire life time*

To facilitate an in-depth and systematic analysis of achievements, I have found it useful to use the theoretical structure provided by Ford (1992). From Ford's perspective, achievements can be analyzed with respect to the following factors:

1. **Goals:** what the person was trying to accomplish;

2. **Emotions:** the accompanying feelings through all aspects of the achievement process;

3. **Personal Agency:** beliefs about one's ability to influence people and situations;

4. **Skills:** learned abilities to do things well;

5. **Context:** personal and situational variables that support or impede goal attainment;

6. **Biological Capacity:** physical capabilities to carry out particular tasks.

These factors serve as guidelines for interpreting achievements, they also can be used as a source for stimulating questions about particular aspects of an achievement. For example, if a client were to describe an achievement with little reference to feelings, you might ask a specific question about feelings associated with the achievement.

In terms of general use of an achievement profiling approach, I believe that the Ford (1992) system represents only one example of how this type of profiling can be applied. It's thoroughness is an advantage but also may not fit some situations. Even when you cannot do the complete evaluation, there is still something to be gained by using a more limited approach. The Career Pathways booklet that was described earlier uses one activity where two achievements are analyzed as part of a skill identification exercise. This activity has a more limited focus and has proven to be a valuable career exploration tool. Another variation of the study of achievements is used in the Starting Points Program (Westwood, Amundson, & Borgen, 1994). With this approach, one achievement is broadly analyzed as a basis for acquiring a better understanding of skills, interests, personality traits, values and support from others.

Career Anchors (Values)

According to Schein (1992), people define themselves in relation to their work using what he has termed "career anchors." "A person's career anchor is the evolving self-concept of what one is good at, what one's needs and motives are, and what values govern one's work related choices. One does not have a career anchor until one has worked for a number of years and has had relevant feedback from those experiences. But once a career anchor evolves, roughly five to ten years after one has started work, it becomes a stabilizing force in the total personality that guides and constrains future career choices." (pp. 207-208) Using a longitudinal research approach, Schein (1992) has defined the following career anchors:

> *A person's career anchor is the evolving self-concept of what one is good at, what one's needs and motives are, and what values govern one's work related choices.*

1. **Security/Stability**: A desire to achieve economic security and stability. Considerable focus is placed on job "tenure," benefit packages, and retirement plans. People with this anchor place a considerable emphasis upon careful planning for the future.

2. **Autonomy/Independence**: A desire for personal control over all forms of regimentation (dress codes, hours of work, rules, routines) associated with many types of work. People with this anchor like to set their own course of actions and are resistant to all attempts to curb freedoms.

3. **Technical or Functional Competence**: This perspective is closely tied to the development of particular talents or skills. People with this anchor are keenly interested in challenging themselves to reach their full potential in a well-defined area of expertise.

4. **General Management Competence**: The focus here is upon general management skills which enable the person to run the organization. With this view, people use a wide range of skills (interpersonal, technical, analytical) to manage the organization and define themselves through organizational successes.

5. **Entrepreneurial Creativity**: With this anchor there is a desire to create a business, product or service. The basic need here is to create something new which is an extension of oneself. Making money is one of the associated values, but it is not necessarily an end in itself.

6. **Service/Dedication to a Cause**: People with this anchor see their careers as a means to fulfil some core values. There often is a strong desire to make the world a better place to live.

7. **Pure Challenge**: From this perspective there is a constant desire to challenge oneself with difficult situations. Competition is often associated with this anchor.

8. **Life Style**: People with this anchor are interested in balance and in integrating work accomplishments with family commitments and personal growth needs. They are willing to sacrifice some work advancements in order to meet their overall needs.

These career anchors bear some similarities to a broad conceptualization of work values put forward by Plant (1997) According to some ethnographic work in Denmark, people approach their work from one of the following three perspectives:

1. **Wage Earner**: Concerned with making a good living and leading a balanced life style. In many respects the categories of Security/ Stability and Life Style would seem to fit with this perspective.

2. **Careerist**: Dedicated to one's profession with a willingness to engage in ongoing learning and professional development. The categories of Technical or Functional Competence, General Management Competence, Service/Dedication to a Cause and possibly Pure Challenge would seem to fit here.

3. **Entrepreneur**: Focused on creating new enterprises and creating new products. The category of Entrepreneurial Creativity is a natural fit, and one could also make the case for Autonomy/Independence.

Using the category system of either Schein (1992) or Plant (1997), you can facilitate an interesting exploration of basic career values and personality attributes. In working with both of these systems, I have found it helpful to have clients identify their most significant career anchors (values) but to be somewhat flexible with this task. Some people are very clear in making their designations (rank ordering), while others have more difficulty making definitive choices. These differences may simply be a reflection of different personality styles. The main point is the discussion of motivating principles and it is toward this end that attention is directed.

To facilitate the discussion process around certain key career anchors (values), I have found it helpful to use the following interviewing process. After allowing people an opportunity to make their initial assessments, I encourage further discussion by enquiring about examples where they were able to apply their desired anchor(s) or were frustrated in their attempts to do so. Following this examination of "contrasts," the discussion shifts to a more "developmental" perspective concerning how the particular anchor developed over time, i.e. has the person always been as focused on a particular anchor and what has been the impact of changing life circumstances. Lastly, the "context" is further explored by examining the consistency of career anchor preferences with current life and career choices. This comprehensive exploration process helps to elaborate various facets of the preferred career anchors (values) and these insights can be applied to new situations.

Card Sorts

Throughout the counselling process, there are times when clients are faced with the task of selecting their significant values, interests, skills, personality traits, and ultimately, occupational options. During this process, it is not uncommon for clients to start with a number of options and then, through a rank ordering process, highlight those aspects which are most applicable. The activities described earlier in the Career Pathways program illustrate this method of selection.

To facilitate the sorting process, I have found it helpful to utilize cards to represent the various elements. When I make the task more tactile, clients have the opportunity to move physically the various options until they are satisfied with the results. This concrete procedure requires a little more preparatory work, but the results are usually well worth the time and effort.

Through experience, I have found that it is difficult for many clients to arrive at an absolute rank order. It is often helpful to break the task down into several steps. For example, suppose that a client is looking at a list of interests. Each of the interests could be placed on a card and the first task would be to identify those that seem to apply and those that don't (with a separate category for those in the undecided realm). During this process, the client would be encouraged to talk about their rationale for the various choices. In a situation where there are many interests, it may be necessary to do a second sort where clients are asked to select their top ten interests. Following this, a pyramid schema might be used as the basis for a further selection (one at the top, two selections at the second level, three selections at the third level and the

By making the task more tactile, clients have the opportunity to move physically the various options until they are satisfied with the results.

remaining four selections at the bottom level). In a situation where very few interests are noted by a client, it may be necessary to go back into the pile of undecided interests to see if additional choices might be added. The purpose of the exercise is to facilitate decision making and to better understand some of the underlying reasons for the choices that are being made by the client.

Occupational card sorts have received considerable attention in the literature (Gysbers & Moore, 1987) and are a very effective means of dealing with occupational information. If you are developing your own card sort system, it is important to use a wide selection of occupations. In a particular counselling session, you may only use fifty or sixty cards which are appropriate for a client, but your overall list may include up to two hundred different occupations.

When you are selecting a range of occupations, it is important to keep in mind the educational level of the various options as well as the different types of occupations. John Holland's (1985a) personality and environmental types can be a useful way to organize occupational choices to ensure that you have a sufficiently comprehensive selection. Using this system occupations can be classified using the following six categories:

Realistic: Involves working with tools, animals, or in an outdoor setting.

Investigative: Involves investigating, understanding, and solving problems.

Artistic: Involves use of imagination and creativity to make new ideas.

Social: Involves helping, informing, and training people.

Enterprising: Involves influencing, persuading, and managing people.

Conventional: Involves working with data, numbers, and carrying out details.
(Gysbers and Moore, p. 133)

Particular occupations fall under more than one category and are usually described using a three-letter code. For example, the occupation "counsellor" has the code SAE which illustrates its connection to the social, artistic and enterprising categories.

Information about particular occupations can be located in a number of different publications. On the cards you only have room to give a short description of the occupation, but it is also helpful to give some code information so that clients can conduct their own more extensive research at a later date. Thus the two codes which might be listed include Holland's classification and a code from a reference system such as Job Futures or the Dictionary of Occupational Titles (more information on these and other source materials is available in the next chapter).

The cards themselves usually have the name of the occupation on the one side and the other descriptive information on the other side, i.e. brief description, Holland code, other codes from Job Futures. Gysbers and Moore (1987) recommend using 3 by 5 inch cards.

When clients are making choices, they usually focus just on the titles at the start, knowing that they can turn the cards over if they want more information. As a starting point, clients are encouraged to go through the cards quickly, sorting them into three piles (Like, Dislike, Undecided). Following this initial sort there is time to look more carefully at what has been selected and the particular themes that might be evident. Listing the various Holland codes is one way to look at the types of areas that are most common. Along with listing the information, I have found it helpful to focus specifically on the reasons being given for the various selections. To focus this discussion, start by simply writing down the reasons the client gives for the occupations chosen and also for those that have been placed in the Dislike and Undecided categories. A flipchart can be helpful at this point for recording the information and for helping to identify major themes.

After the initial sort of occupations and the discussion about possible themes, it can be useful to prioritize the occupations. As was mentioned earlier, it is often desirable to use no more than ten occupations and the pyramid schema is a good way to have them arranged. Once this information has been generated, clients can be encouraged to do further research on these and other related occupations, by using the codes that have been given as a guide.

Card sorts using values are also quite common and can be a useful means of generating reflection and discussion. Values can be considered from at least two different levels. On the one hand, there are values that point to broadly based considerations, such as good health, social status, serving others, truth, spirituality, and so on. Other more specific values might address issues of creativity, variety, working conditions and achievement. Mossop (1994) distinguishes between the general and the more specific values using the terms "guiding" and "practical" values. As with the occupational card sorts, the task is to develop a set of cards with different value statements on each card. The task then is to sort the values into those domains that are most prominent and those that are less so, with an undecided category for those values where there is some uncertainty. To facilitate the selection process, I have often found it helpful to give clients a target with respect to how many values should find their way into the most desired pile—no more than ten top values. The total number of value cards may vary, but a deck of from forty to fifty cards is common. Of course, once the task is completed, the emphasis is upon discussing how the choices were made and how these values play a part in their career decision making.

The Early Years

There is little doubt that we are heavily influenced by our early experiences in our families, with our friends, and at school. While I don't want to move in an overly psychodynamic direction with "deep" interpretations, there is some value in having clients look at early influences and reflect upon how these events might impact their current career conceptions.

Savickas (1997) describes a career counselling method based on the analysis of early recollections. With this approach, clients are instructed to think back to three of their earliest memories. As with other methods, such as the pattern identification exercise or achievement profiling, there is the belief that contained within the stories are basic personal elements which reflect life themes. The goal is to help clients discern these themes so that they can use the information with their decision making. Identifying themes can present a challenge, and Savickas (1997) describes a process whereby he has clients write headlines for the various stories. These headlines serve as reference points for the stories and help to clarify the major aspects of the life themes.

there is some value in having clients look at early influences and reflect upon how these events might impact their current career conceptions

In my own practice, I have used early recollections but have not sought to restrict the memories to those that are "earliest." My focus has been on memories throughout the life span. I believe that there are multiple memories that could be explored for meaningful information. The main point is that the memories are significant to the person. I would speculate that each age period would likely contain important memories that reflect certain life themes. For persons interested in general life review, it would be important to tap into memories during different time periods.

Another approach to early influences is to examine the advice that people have been given along the way. There seems to be no shortage of advice, and it is interesting to focus on some of the messages that were given by family members, friends, and others, such as teachers or prominent individuals. The giving of advice is important to acknowledge, whether it is stated verbally or simply implied through the actions of others. The important point here, however, is to look not only at what advice was being given but also how it was being received. After asking clients to identify the advice they have received from different sources, I always follow-up with the question, "*And what were you thinking and feeling when you heard this piece of advice?*" The "self talk" of clients helps to affirm or discount the advice that was given.

The influence of others is realized at many different levels. Savickas (1997) points to the importance of role models and suggests that these special people "'serve as templates that individuals use to design their own lives" (p. 14). Asking clients about the people they admire can lead to important insights about their values and interests. I would suggest that alongside these "heroes" there are also "dragons" that might be useful to explore. As the flip side of the coin, these negative models can also play a role in determining life themes.

For persons interested in general life reviews, it would be important to tap into memories during different time periods.

Summary

The self-assessment tasks described in this chapter, while non-standardized, are systematic and do follow a structured enquiry process. Specific questions are asked to further self-exploration and in some instances relevant information is provided. The advantage of this type of systematic organizing framework is that while the tasks are relatively straightforward, they can lead in some interesting directions. To get full value from the tasks you will need to leave yourself open to following some of the unexpected directions that might emerge.

The next chapter continues with the self-assessment theme but focuses on more dynamic counselling tasks. These activities are less structured and counsellors must be ready to move forward within a more ambiguous context.

CHAPTER 5

PROBLEM
RESOLVING
TASKS:

Dynamic Self-Assessment

This chapter continues with the focus on self-assessment but addresses this issue with more dynamic problem resolving tasks. The activities presented are dynamic in the sense that there is less structure for the counsellor-client dialogue. Within this more ambiguous framework, there certainly is a major emphasis upon creativity and imagination (on the part of clients as well as counsellors).

If you are planning to use some of these more dynamic strategies, you may find that they are more challenging. Training and experience will help you to more fully appreciate the underlying personal dynamics of your clients as well as yourself. Learning to trust your own intuitive feelings will also help you with these tasks.

Mind Mapping

The working of the human mind is interesting to reflect upon. The right and left hemispheres provide us with very different types of experience. From the left side, we seem to acquire our abilities to define and sequence activities logically. The right, on the other hand, brings forth our more creative capacities and concerns itself with images and patterns. Both hemispheres make important contributions and mind mapping is concerned with trying to capture some of the thought patterns of the right hemisphere.

There are a number of ways in which mind mapping can be applied. The most basic involves "brainstorming," where the task is simply getting ideas down on paper without evaluating them. It requires a non-judgmental attitude and a willingness to let our minds drift towards any and all solutions. The advantage of using this approach is that it makes room for the innovative ideas which otherwise might never come forward because of preconceived notions. Once the ideas have been generated, they can then be evaluated with respect to their possible utility.

the focus here is to let your creative thoughts take over for awhile and to look for interesting and novel connections

Another form of mind mapping uses a type of "clustering" to generate a wider range of possibilities. Lusser Rico (1983) describes the general principles of clustering as follows:

> To create a cluster, you begin with a nucleus word, circled, on a fresh page. Now you simply let go and begin to flow with any current of connections that come into your head. Write these down rapidly, each in its own circle,

radiating outward from the center in any direction they
want to go. Connect each new word or phrase with a line
to the preceding circle. When something new and
different strikes you, begin again at the central nucleus
and radiate outward until those associations are
exhausted... Continue to cluster, drawing lines and even
arrows to associations that seem to go together, but don't
dwell on what goes where. Let each association find its
own place. If you momentarily run out of associations,
doodle a bit by filling in arrows or making lines darker.
(pp. 35-36)

As with brainstorming, the focus here is to let your creative thoughts
take over for awhile and to look for interesting and novel connections.
This type of clustering activity can be particularly helpful when looking
at either barriers or strengths. With barriers, the emphasis is on the
identification of different coping strategies. With strengths, there can be a
reinforcement and expansion of perceived strengths.

I also have used a form of mind mapping as a way of summarizing
what has been covered during a counselling session. This can be
particularly appropriate in situations where it feels that you have been "all
over the map." When counsellors find themselves drifting without a sense
of direction, it can be helpful to take a few moments to reflect upon the
territory that has been covered. To do this, I have found it helpful to use a
flip chart as a basis for constructing a map of what has been discussed. To
start, think about the major themes that have been mentioned and place
them on the page. Then, with each one, draw out some of the minor
points and look for any new connections that might emerge. I have found
that in many instances, just seeing the topics spread out in this fashion
helps the counsellor to formulate some new patterns and also to set a
direction for future discussions.

Audio/Video Playback

Clients are often unaware of how they are "coming across" during counselling sessions and seem to lack perspective with respect to their own interpersonal behaviour. Talking about these discrepancies can lead to some insight, but often the most effective approach is to use audio or video recording to play back to the client certain clips reflecting their behaviour in counselling sessions.

The first reaction from clients to this type of direct feedback is usually surprise at hearing and viewing themselves through this medium. After the initial responses to what may seem a novelty, there is the opportunity to explore certain behaviours. For example, clients may use story telling or tangents to keep you at an emotional distance.

> *With this medium, client defensiveness can be reduced and there can be an increased willingness to directly address issues.*

By isolating some specific examples of this type of behaviour, you have the opportunity to address problems directly using concrete illustrations. The audio/video clips allow you and your clients the opportunity to evaluate behaviours from a different perspective (externalization). With this medium, client defensiveness can be reduced and there can be an increased willingness to directly address issues.

Audio/video playback also can play an important role in reflecting some of the gains that have been realized through the counselling process. In one recent situation, a client came to counselling feeling very discouraged. This despair was reflected in his voice, his non-verbal actions (not looking at the counsellor) and the way in which he was dressed. Over a period of time, he began to talk with more authority; he cut his hair and was obviously putting more effort into his self care. These changes could be reflected to him through a process of comparing current video tape segments with some of the earlier tapes. In this respect then, the audio/video playback strategy helped to reinforce the positive changes that had been attained.

In this way, the use of audio/video equipment tends to allow a certain reflectiveness in the counselling session. There also are ways in which audio/video playback can be actively incorporated into the learning process. In the next chapter there is a section on behavioural rehearsal strategies which focuses on how clients can learn through role playing various interviewing and job search strategies. Audio/video playback can be an important part of this learning strategy. As clients role play new behaviours, they can record their actions and play back the segments to consolidate their learning through a constructive feedback model.

I believe that we are just starting to realize the many ways in which we could creatively incorporate technology into our counselling sessions for added effectiveness. The use of audio/video recording and playback seems to be restricted primarily to job search groups. Nevertheless with advances in technology and the increasing emphasis upon accountability, it is not hard to imagine a scenario where the use of recordings and playback will become standard practice.

Two- and Three-Chair Resolution of "Splits"

During the process of defining the various aspects of problems, clients often find themselves torn between two different perspectives. Some typical examples include those who feel at one level that it is a time for a change but, on the other hand, have certain responsibilities to consider. Others might be more internally focused and want to do something different but feel constrained by personal inadequacies. And then there are those who are plagued by indecision where one part of them wants to move in a certain direction but another part has very different desires. These splits lead to agitation and confusion and cry out for some form of resolution.

> *clients are encouraged to move from simply "talking about" the different issues to "acting out" the various positions–a way to externalize issues and begin the resolution process.*

One way of resolving splits is to use a procedure of dramatic re-enactment using chairs to represent the different parts of the self (Greenberg, Rice and Elliott, 1993). With this procedure, clients are encouraged to move from simply "talking about" the different issues to "acting out" the various positions–a way to externalize issues and begin the resolution process. This activity can take some time and it is important to initiate the activity when there is no particular time press. From my experience, this type of enactment usually takes at least a half hour to complete.

When setting up the actual procedure, you will need to give clients some direction as it often can be a little awkward at the beginning. The two chairs represent the different competing perspectives; when clients sit in the respective chairs, they are asked to assume fully the posture and identity of each position. For example, if one chair represents the breaking free and moving in a new direction part of themselves, they need to be encouraged to fully take on the excitement and freedom that comes with that position. When they are sitting in the other chair, they may be feeling angry and dismayed by the irresponsibility that is being contemplated; this too needs to be expressed both verbally and non-verbally. Helping clients to find their "voices" in each of the chairs is an important part of the process. In some situations, it may be useful in the beginning to have clients exaggerate the various roles in order to engage more fully in the role playing activity. Another start-up problem is the extent to which clients are willing to direct their comments to the other empty chair rather than to the counsellor. In some instances, it is simply a matter of instructing clients to talk to the other chair. If this persists as a problem, it can be helpful for the counsellor to move to a position behind or to the side of the client and continue directing the client to address their comments to the empty chair. Naming the two chairs can also be important. When choosing names, I have tried to use the names that the clients are using when referring to the various positions, for example, the responsible versus the risk-taking self.

> *Using dramatic re-enactment to handle splits is not an assurance that problems will be resolved. It usually does, however, better clarify the positions and in many instances can lead to significant resolutions.*

Usually at the beginning, the two sides that are being represented do not have equal power and status. Greenberg, Rice and Elliott (1993) refer to the chairs using the terminology "top-dog" and "under-dog." The conflict that is initially portrayed is usually one where the top-dog chair is leveling some criticisms at the other position and the under-dog chair is responding with more affective reactions to the criticisms. I have found it helpful to help clients frame their comments from both chairs in terms of feelings as well as content.

During the two-chair exercise, you need to assume the role of director and at certain points move the client from one chair to the next. Determining the best moment when to make the switch can be a challenge and requires careful attention to the ongoing dialogue. In most instances, it is necessary to move clients back and forth several times in order to articulate the two positions fully.

The interesting part of the back-and-forth movement is that clients often begin to experience change as the dialogue continues. At some point, the under-dog may speak out more forcefully or the top-dog begins to soften . Whatever the process, there can be a coming together of the two chairs into a more unified and integrated whole. Part of the difficulty for many counsellors is waiting for this shift in perspective to occur. It is normal in many instances to go through a somewhat stormy period before this resolution occurs. I have found it helpful in some instances to move the chairs closer together to reflect this change in position. Again, the more concrete you can make the situation, the more significant the impact becomes.

It would be misleading to suggest that all splits lead to happy conclusions after a period of back-and-forth dialogue. There are times when the sides just don't seem to be moving toward resolution. At such times, I have introduced a third chair, a mediator chair, where clients step outside of their problem and try to find some type of mediated solution. In this more neutral stance, clients search for some form of creative way of bringing the two sides together (at least closer together). When clients are sitting in this mediator chair, you should feel free to contribute to the search for some means of reconciling the two positions.

Using dramatic re-enactment to handle splits is not an assurance that problems will be resolved. It usually does, however, better clarify the positions and in many instances can lead to significant resolutions. The power of the enactment can be very significant; and, when using this approach, you should be ready to cope with any affective reactions which might accompany the dialogue, i.e. have a tissue box handy.

Following the completion of the split chair activity, there is usually a need to debrief what transpired. As with other debriefings, clients are encouraged to discuss what they experienced and you can also add your perspective. In some instances the two-chair split may need to be continued at some later time.

Greenberg, Rice and Elliott (1993) have described the two-chair process using the following stages:

1. **Predialogue Stage**

   A collaborative discussion with the client about the structure of the two-chair activity and the respective roles of the counsellor and client.

2. **Opposition Stage**

   Identifying the two aspects of the self and then separating them by using the two chairs. Facilitating a dialogue between the two sides where responsibility is assumed for each side's position,

3. **Contact Stage**

   Helping clients to become aware of automatic self-criticisms and injunctions (use of words such as "should," "must," "have to"). Increasing the specificity of the client's self-criticisms and injunctions. Helping the client to access and experience the accompanying emotions and needs. Helping the client to become aware of values and standards.

4. **Integration Stage**

   Promoting the expression of mutually supportive feelings and "softening" actions. Facilitating negotiation or integration.

5. **Postdialogue Stage**

Creating perspective and better understanding of the situation. Helping clients to reflect upon their experience.

These stages help to describe the process, but they also need to be viewed with flexibility. As mentioned earlier, there are occasions when integration does not fully occur, but you can still help clients through the debriefing to develop some new insights on the problem.

Multiple Perspectives

The two-chair strategy that has just been discussed externalizes the problem by using chairs to separate different parts of the self. This same idea can be used in other ways, for example, breaking the self into multiple parts and then facilitating a dialogue between the various elements. In making these somewhat arbitrary distinctions, you can use various types of categories as vantage points from which to view the issue under consideration.

the emphasis with this method is on building new insights through having people shift their perspectives

Because of the multiple perspectives that are being represented in the discussion, it is often not practical to use chairs to represent the various elements. Gelatt (1991) has suggested using Edward de Bono's (1985) "imaginary thinking hats" to reflect the different options and, to my mind, this seems like a good option. One could, for example, use different pencil crayons to symbolize the various positions. When a person was speaking from a particular position, they would hold the pencil crayon associated with that particular viewpoint.

The six imaginary thinking hats correspond to the following schema:

White - Objective	Yellow - Positive
Red - Emotional	Green - Creative
Black - Negative	Blue - Controlling

When people assume one of the hats, they view the problem from a particular perspective. They are encouraged to assess the problem fully from each of the hats and then discuss the insights that come to them.

Another way of formulating perspectives is by using the First Nations Medicine Wheel as a schema (McCormick and Amundson, 1997). With this approach, the problem is viewed from four vantage points. There are the Cognitive, Emotional, Behavioural and Spiritual perspectives and they all need to be taken into account. Problem resolution is only found through achieving satisfaction in each of these realms. This satisfaction is grounded in the belief that balance needs to be achieved when solving problems. It is not enough to find the best rational decision to a problem; the solution must also fit with emotional, behavioural, and spiritual needs. The Medicine Wheel schema divides the self for analytical purposes; but, ultimately, the pieces must be put together into an integrated whole.

There are undoubtedly many other ways that one could categorize various perspectives on a problem. One might use time as an organizer and look at issues from the perspective of past, present and future. Location might also serve as an organizer. For example, if someone was imagining leaving an area for a job in another location, they might take their various options and use these as vantage points for assessing the viability of each position. A final method of organization might be construed around the concept of continuum. With this perspective, there is a focus on magnitude and this can be applied to various situations. For example, a person might be looking at further education and considering related options which take varying amounts of time (e.g. one year, three years, five years) to complete. The options might also vary in terms of the degree of effort and skill required to complete the requirements.

Whatever the system of categorization that is used, the emphasis with this method is on building new insights through having people shift their perspectives. As I stated earlier, many clients find themselves "stuck in a rut" and are looking for ways to view their situation from other perspectives. These exercises are designed to facilitate this type of movement and can hopefully lead to some new insights.

Metaphors and Symbols

As was indicated in Chapter Three, metaphors are excellent ways of capturing the essential elements of the problem as perceived by the client. With a few simple images, at least some aspects of the problem can be defined. Other ways to illustrate aspects of the problem include using symbols to represent various parts of the problem. An empty bottle may signify a relationship to alcohol, a rejection letter for the many rejections one has experienced during unemployment, a certificate of achievement for accomplishments, and so on. Whether one is using a symbol such as an empty bottle or a metaphoric image of the situation, the effect is similar. People become more focused with problem definition and there is a bringing together of a wealth of information under one image.

The challenge during this phase of the counselling process is not only to define the problem but also to move beyond it and seek new solutions. Thus, the self-assessment task becomes one of developing alternate images or symbols to reflect a new reality. In some instances, this may involve working with the client's image; in other situations a totally new image might be introduced.

One way to change metaphors is to introduce the notion of time (past, present and future) into the structure that has been created, i.e. what it was like before, what it is like now, and what you are hoping for the future. The "miracle question" that was described earlier often incorporates a visualization where there is an excellent opportunity to use some metaphoric imagery (future-focused, where clients see themselves at some point in time). Using time-sequenced drawings, clients are able to see themselves at various points on a

metaphors are excellent ways of capturing the essential elements of the problem as perceived by the client.

continuum. Viewing the past, moving to the present, and then onward to the future allows clients to see how events are changing and also to think about some of the steps that serve to connect the various images, in particular, what steps need to be taken in order to arrive at the future focused destination.

Another way to structure this process is to use the strategy outlined by Vahamottonen, Keskinen and Parrila (1994). With this approach, clients are asked to imagine their present circumstances and some possible future developments. They are then given a large sheet of paper with the words "Me Here and Now" written in the centre of the page. They are asked to develop a drawing which includes whatever has come to their minds, with particular emphasis on the themes and persons that they felt were relevant to their situation. The drawing usually includes a number of metaphoric images (example: ball represents their involvement in sports), and you can use these images as a starting point for discussing their current situation and what they see as possible solutions.

the self-assessment task becomes one of developing alternate images to reflect a new reality; this may involve working with the client's image or a totally new image might be introduced

When you develop alternate metaphors and symbols for clients, it is important to keep in mind how the images might be received. For example, sporting images might be appropriate for some people but not for others. It is essential to develop images which fit within the life context of the person. In a recent counselling situation, I was working with a young First Nations student who was considering various educational and career opportunities. He was very gifted and had the desire to move forward with his aspirations. On the other hand, he felt some obligations for leadership to the people on his reserve. In giving him a metaphor, I used the image of the land (an important value in First Nations culture) and also addressed the role of leadership through the following metaphor:

"I see you moving out of your community; breaking, a path through some newly fallen snow. It is hard work breaking the path and you have to keep your eyes fixed on the goal ahead so that you can keep going. Some others in the community are watching you take these steps and are deciding whether to follow behind."

Through this concrete image, he was able to see that he could combine his educational and vocational aspirations with his desire for leadership. He began to realize that leading by example was perhaps the truest form of leadership.

In another situation, one of the counsellors I recently worked with brought a hockey puck into the counselling session when working with a client who was depressed and also very interested in NHL hockey. Much of the discussion focused on how problems could be viewed as an opposing hockey team (externalization) and, of course, there were ways to defend against the opposition (negative self talk) and to become offensive when the opportunities arose (becoming an agent rather than a pawn). The symbol of the puck served as a concrete reminder of the hockey metaphor, and the client seemed to enjoy holding it when discussing problems and potential solutions.

Metaphors serve as important tools at each step of the counselling process. They can also be a very visible reminder of the successes that have been achieved. Regular use of metaphors provides counsellors with a clear record of the transition process.

Learning Through Games

Group situations offer a wonderful opportunity to develop new insights through participation in "games." Games often mirror the realities of life and, as such, tend to be a useful type of metaphor within the counselling setting. These games are designed to be fun but also to offer valuable insights through debriefing the interpersonal interchanges and individual reactions within the context of the game. Many trainers use games to get a point across. For example, when discussing change, people may be asked to clasp their hands together in the way that feels most comfortable. Some people will have their right thumb on top and others their left. When asked to reverse their grip, they will notice an appreciable difference, i.e. not as comfortable. In discussing the situation, you can make the point that there are differences in the positions that people find comfortable, when change occurs there is a disruption to the system and it can be difficult to adjust to new circumstances.

> *Games often mirror the realities of life, and as such, tend to be a useful type of metaphor within the counselling setting.*

Another activity that I have used when talking about change is to fill glasses of water at random during the course of the time that I am with the group without saying anything about what I am doing (Fritz, 1991). Clients soon start to try to interpret what is going on and eventually will demand to know what is happening. Before providing my rationale, I ask for their speculations. Usually there are a number of interesting possibilities, i.e. "*you put water in the glasses when we ask a good question*" or "*you fill the glasses at the end of each section.*" In fact, the main reason for filling the glasses is to make the point that you can't always understand everything that is happening. We often find ourselves scrambling to decode information which just doesn't make sense. There are times when we need to let the unknown remain a mystery and be content in the moment, not understanding what is happening.

Other more elaborate games with groups can be set up to address issues of teamwork and learning styles. One such game that I have used on many occasions involves the building of paper airplanes. I initially break the group into small groups (4 - 6 persons) and then assign them the task of building airplanes for a contest to see who can come closest to a target on the other side of the room. The rules are such that each team member has to throw at least one airplane. I usually ask each team to throw a few more airplanes than their actual numbers (to see who gets to throw more than one airplane and how this is decided). Thus, if there are five people on a team, they might throw a total of eight airplanes. The airplanes have to fly on the wind currents and cannot be simply a crumpled ball of paper. To add to the fun, there is an individual prize for the person throwing the winning airplane and a group prize for the team that he/she is representing, i.e. a chocolate bar for the person and some peanuts for the group. During the activity, the various teams take turns in throwing their airplanes and the tension mounts. At the end of the activity, I ask the groups to come together to review their experience during the course of the game. Some of the questions for debriefing this game are as follows:

1. How did your group go about devising a plan for building airplanes? What strategies were employed and how did various people fit within this scenario, i.e. were there any leaders, how were decisions made, what did you learn from your experiences?

2. What types of self-talk were evident during the game? What was the nature of the relationship between those with knowledge about paper airplane making and those who had few skills?

3. What happened during the actual throwing of the airplanes? What group feelings and discussion characterized each stage of the activity?

Following this small group discussion, the groups are brought together for a broader discussion of how insights from this activity can be applied to individual learning styles, motivation, decision making, group teamwork and so on.

In applying these game activities, you need to have a clear purpose in mind. The games do serve to energize the group, but usually there needs to be some other motivation for doing the activity. The use of games needs to be placed carefully with the phases of group development in mind. If there is insufficient group cohesion, members may resist participating in an activity where there is some ambiguity about the final result. Obviously the point of the game is to draw people into some "real life" experiences where they respond in certain ways and then reflect upon the actions they have taken. Engaging in this type of activity involves some risk taking and there is a need for some initial group bonding to establish trust in the group and in the leader.

Many different types of games can be applied for learning purposes. The main point is to choose games which are appropriate for the level of group development and which lead to some interesting interpersonal experiences. Leaving sufficient time for debriefing is also essential so that the full value of the activity can be realized.

While the impact of games is considerable in a group context, I have also found that games can be effectively used within individual counselling sessions. For example, clients can be challenged with various puzzles to help them develop their creative thinking abilities. Some of the insights derived from these activities can be applied to career problem solving. As with games in a group setting, it is important that you leave enough time for debriefing at the end of the activity.

Writing and Poetry

The emphasis in this chapter on self reflection is something that occurs both within and outside of counselling sessions. One of the ways to meet this goal is to encourage clients and counsellors to reflect upon their experiences using writing and poetry. Writing can take many different forms, i.e. recording daily events, journal writing, letter writing, and free expression. Many people enjoy writing prose or poetry and find that it helps them with their understanding of themselves and situations.

The power of writing can be felt at many different levels. At its most basic, it can simply be a recording of present events. Often people don't realize certain behavioural patterns until they are recorded. Taking note of the various activities during a typical day has a way of focusing attention on what is happening as well as what is not happening. People who are coping with unemployment or with burnout at work can attain some important insights by carefully examining what is occurring over the course of a day.

> *The power of writing can be felt at many different levels.*

Writing can also be personally expressive and in this mode the keeping of journal entries focused on the counselling process can be helpful. With a journal, clients can record their thoughts and feelings about occurrences during counselling sessions–a form of mental review. They can also look at other experiences outside of counselling and reflect on how they are applying what they have been learning. Thus, the journal record becomes more than just a focus for the counselling sessions; it also becomes a reflection of the impact counselling is having in other areas of their lives. For example, if they are involved in job search, they might want to examine their thoughts and feelings as they contact employers. If they are at the career exploration stage, they will need to reflect upon their experiences as they acquire additional information about possible career fields.

The working out of problems can occur at a semi-conscious level with the creative process serving as a powerful driving force. Unharnessing creative energy usually serves as a useful resource for resolving counselling problems whether directly or indirectly.

You can assign to clients specific homework activities which lend themselves to journal writing. At the beginning of Chapter Four, there was the discussion of various questioning techniques. Some of the questions focused on pre-session changes, coping in other situations and exception finding. While these are certainly valid areas to pursue within a counselling session, they are also topics that clients could address in their journal writing. With the support of a collaborative relationship, clients need to consider their personal strengths both within and outside of the counselling situation.

Writing letters is also something that counsellors can do to reflect upon the dynamics of the counselling process. Under some circumstances, these writings can be shared with clients. White and Epston (1990) describe a process where a number of different types of letters (invitation, redundancy, prediction and so on) can be written to clients as one form of communication. Vahamottonen (1998) illustrates this letter writing technique in a career counselling situation where there is an impasse with respect to moving forward with a career decision. Rather than chastizing the client for her lack of movement, he commends her for carefully considering her options before acting (a strength challenge perspective). The following is a portion of the letter that was sent to the client:

> "...I admire your capacity to enjoy your life stage at this moment. I think that most people in your position would rush into making solutions which they would later regret. But instead, you think things over from different perspectives very

*carefully. When the time comes you will make your decision,
and the decision will be a successful one because you have
thought it through so carefully."* (p. 68)

By using this strategy, Vahamottonen was able to reframe the lack of
action and consider the situation from a new perspective. This particular
client was very self determined and wasn't about to be pushed into
making a quick decision. By focusing on her ability to decide for herself
when the time was right, he reinforced her sense of personal agency and
this seemed to be appropriate for the situation.

Another form of writing involves free expression as clients construct
stories and plays. In these dramatizations, it is not uncommon to have
projections about current counselling issues. The working out of
problems can occur at a semi-conscious level with the creative process
serving as a powerful driving force. Unharnessing creative energy usually
serves as a useful resource for resolving counselling problems whether
directly or indirectly.

Writing for clients and counsellors can also take a poetic form. Many
people enjoy capturing their experiences with poetic imagery. One client
after participating in a two-chair strategy went home and constructed a
poem about the experience. Poetry can capture the very essence of
thoughts and feelings and is a medium which is worthy of exploration
under the right circumstances. I have found the following poem by
Robert Frost ("The Road Not Taken") helpful in discussing with clients
some of the tensions associated with career decision making.

The Road Not Taken

Two roads diverged in a yellow wood,
And sorry I could not travel both
And be one traveller, long I stood
And looked down one as far as I could
To where it bent in the undergrowth

Then took the other, as just as fair,
And having perhaps the better claim,
Because it was grassy and wanted wear;
Though as for that the passing there
Had worn them really about the same,

And both that morning equally lay
In leaves no step had trodden blank.
Oh, I kept the first for another day!
Yet knowing how way leads on to way,
I doubted if I should ever come back.
I shall do this with a sigh
Somewhere ages and ages hence;
Two roads diverged in a wood, and I
took the one less travelled by
And that has made all the difference!

Projective Methods

The term "projective" refers to the general process of extension, casting forward, and so on. As we interact with the world, we perceive events based on our own particular needs and personal characteristics. Our projective stance influences how we take in information and how we respond to new situations. As an illustration, consider a situation where two people are sitting down in a restaurant, one an instructor from a culinary arts program in a local college and the other a visitor from out of town. As they peruse the menu, it is not hard to imagine that they might be viewing the situation from very different perspectives, i.e. price, presentation, uniqueness of food items, and so on. Even though the stimulus (the menu) is fairly straightforward, the way it might be perceived bears a strong relationship to the participants' personal projections. With other more ambiguous situations, the differences in perspective might be even more dramatic.

> *Our projective stance influences how we take in information and how we respond to new situations.*

Assessment methods based on the concept of projection have a long history in the psychological literature. These methods (inkblots, drawings, stories, and so on) were initially put forward during the 1930's and 40's as a counter balance to the growing popularity of standardized assessment . The following quotation by Murphy (1947) illustrates how the projective element found its way into the assessment process:

> The term projective methods has come into general use in recent years to denote the devices that enable the subject to project himself in a planned situation. He sees in it what he personally is disposed to see, or does with it what he personally is disposed to do. We are interested

primarily not in the quantity of production, as in an
educational test, but in what he indirectly tells us about
himself through his manner of confronting the task. All
psychological methods involve some projection in the
sense that a person reveals himself in whatever he does.
One may put little, or much, of one's self into a
production; thus the carpenter projects himself when he
makes a doorsill, and to a much greater degree when he
makes a boat. The Allport-Vernon methods are in some
degree projective, the graphological methods still more so,
and the interpretation of ink blots perhaps most
projective of all... Since there is a continuum, the
definition is for convenience only. We shall include under
projection all those methods in which the individual has
full opportunity to live empathetically, that is, in terms of
identification with the material presented to him. (p. 669)

The assessment methods that were developed during these early years
enjoyed initial acceptance but declined in influence in response to some
negative research findings and a failure to move beyond the traditional
medical model. In an earlier article (Amundson, 1979), I made the case
that counsellors may have "thrown the baby out with the bath water"
when retreating from the projective assessment domain. I certainly believe
that some cautions are in order when using projective methods; but in
many ways, I have found a good fit between "informal" projective
assessment methods and career exploration. Having clients respond to
ambiguous stimulus situations can create some interesting productions
and also lead to meaningful discussion and analysis. When working with
these methods, I have found it helpful to stress the collaborative model
that was discussed earlier. As with other strategies, i.e. the PIE, it is often
useful to have the client assume an active role in interpreting the
information. To illustrate some of the possible applications of projective
methods, I will focus on the use of drawings and stories.

1. Drawing Tasks

While I really enjoy working with drawings, I think that it is important as a starting point to acknowledge the fact that this love of drawings is not shared by all clients or counsellors for that matter. Many clients may choose not to participate in a drawing activity for a number of different reasons. I try to encourage participation by assuring people that this task is in no way associated with the judging of artistic merit. Nevertheless, there will still be those who choose not to participate and I respect their wishes. There are many different ways to facilitate projection and perhaps some other methods may be more appropriate i.e. stories.

For those clients who do appreciate this method, there are opportunities for them to illustrate their metaphors with drawings. There also is a place for drawings of the self, other people, and special situations. Listed below are a few illustrations of some typical drawing tasks:

- Using a blank sheet of paper, make a drawing of your present environment. Include in this diagram both the people and places that are important to you. (Modify by having the person look ahead to life in 2 to 5 years time).

- Draw a picture of yourself doing something together with others (Make this drawing more specific by referring to family members, or other significant others).

- Draw a picture of yourself working alone.

- Draw a picture of yourself in your leisure time.

- Draw a picture of yourself working in an '"ideal" work setting.

With each drawing, it is important to ask questions about what is happening in the situation and how the various people are feeling.

Considerable information regarding the interpretation of drawings has been put forward, and I will attempt to summarize some of the information that I have found to be particularly helpful. When you are analyzing drawings, the starting point is always the verbal and non-verbal behaviours associated with completion of the task. You need to ask yourself whether the client was insecure, anxious, suspicious, arrogant, hostile, negative, tense, relaxed, humorous, self-conscious, cautious or impulsive. Also, was any self talk present; and, if so, how was it directed? It is not uncommon to meet people who are uncertain about their artistic talents. What is interesting to observe is how they handle the uncertainty.

The most valid and reliable information usually comes from the identification of general themes. In approaching each drawing, ask questions such as: How does this drawing as a whole impress me? Is it reasonably well structured? What are the essential components? What might lead a person to produce a drawing such as this one? These questions serve to highlight themes in terms of level of organization, level of creativity, relationships with others, relative importance of work-leisure-family, vocational maturity, occupational preference and the emphasis upon people or the physical environment.

> *When you are analyzing drawings, the starting point is always the verbal and non-verbal behaviours associated with completion of the task.*

In addition to the identification of certain general themes, observe the placement of the various people and objects in the diagram. It can be assumed that the closer things are together the stronger the relationship. Thus, if a person were drawing a group of people and placed him/herself on one side of the page and the others in the opposite corner, it would be reasonable to suggest that a relatively weak relationship exists. If, on the other hand, the person was in the middle of the group, a stronger affiliation would be indicated.

The size of a self drawing in relation to the size of the paper can also be an important indicator, particularly in respect to the strength of the self-concept. If someone draws an exceptionally small figure to represent him/herself, this may indicate a depreciation of self worth. An overly large figure, on the other hand, may suggest needs for power and control.

When one compares the size of figures and objects in relation to one another, some further hypotheses in terms of significance can be derived. This is especially the case in situations where an inverse relationship exists between the actual size of people (things) and the size accorded them in the drawing. For example, a dominant parental figure may be drawn two or three times larger than others in the picture.

Graphology also may serve as a significant indicator. You will need to examine both the pressure of the stroke and the rhythm and consider what this might reflect. For example, a very light stroke may be related to inferiority, a choppy stroke to anxiety, a very controlled stroke to rigidity and a fluid motion to expressiveness (Kershaw, 1980). A comprehensive understanding of graphological principles is, of course, a complete study in itself and, although helpful, not essential for the level of interpretation being suggested here.

The use of various colours in drawings also may suggest some preliminary hypotheses. Brower and Weider (1950) suggest that constricted people tend to use fewer colours, people with an effervescent nature shift rapidly from color to color, depressed persons rely more heavily on darker colours and aggressive persons tend to emphasize brighter colours such as red and orange. Color is perhaps the least reliable of the general indicators, but it can prove useful in some instances.

If one examines the human figure (self) in greater detail, some further tentative hypotheses can be derived (Hammer, 1958; Levy, 1950). For instance, the drawing of the head seems related to a person's self concept. A small and poorly defined face may indicate a poor self image. Similarly, if the face has certain cartoon or clown like features this may reflect feelings of inferiority. Other features of the face such as the eyes, nose and teeth also can suggest some hypotheses. For example, the eyes can be expressive or blank, the nose flared (aggressive) or the teeth showing (another sign of aggression). The neck refers to the connecting link between bodily feelings and intellectual thoughts. Absence or distortion of this connection may indicate a lack of integration. The arms and hands are defined as the manipulating organs; and, if they are omitted or distorted, this may suggest difficulties in handling the environment. The feet serve to tie the person to the ground (reality). If they are missing or the person seems to be floating in the air, it may indicate a tendency to be somewhat unrealistic. With the sexual organs, one has to be aware of exaggerations. This may be a sign of sexual dysfunction, but often this simply reflects an attempt to shock the counsellor. In making hypotheses based on this type of information, you need to use considerable caution. As was stated earlier, general patterns are usually more reliable and valid than specific details.

The discussion thus far has centred on interpreting what has been drawn. It is also essential to consider what has been omitted. These omissions may simply reflect a lack of significance, but they can also point to issues of conflict.

To conclude this section on drawings, I think it is important to stress once again the importance of the collaborative relationship in creating hypotheses from drawings. There are many factors that need to be taken into account, and you will need to work with your clients to explore the various facets of drawings. In this exploration, your role is primarily one of asking some open ended questions and facilitating an active exploration of issues.

2. Story Creations

One of the cornerstones of projective methods is the development of stories based on pictures as a stimulus, i.e. the Thematic Apperception Test (TAT). I have found in career counselling that some interesting results can be obtained by using pictures which are current and reflect a variety of career counselling concerns. The custom-made pictures I use touch on issues such as family life, leisure pursuits, job search, and the work environment. While I have developed a large set of pictures over the years, I only start with about ten pictures which I believe to have some personal relevance for the client. As a starting point, there is the request to choose no more than half of the pictures and to use their imagination to develop stories (in written form or with a tape recorder) based on what might be happening. The stories should have a beginning, middle and an end and reflect the feelings and thoughts of the characters involved. The completion of these stories can either be handled within the counselling session or as a homework assignment. Once the person has completed the stories, there should be a discussion of them (further elaboration) and an inquiry about the meaningfulness of the various stories.

Lindzey (1952) has outlined some basic assumptions involved in the analysis of stories:

- In the process of creating a story, the story-teller often identifies with one person. The wishes, strivings and conflicts of this story character may reflect those of the story-teller.

- All of the stories that are created are not of equal importance to the person. Certain crucial stories may be the most revealing.

- Themes or story-elements that appear to have arisen directly out of the pictures are less apt to be significant than those elements that have been added.

- It is important to pay particular attention to recurrent themes.

- The stories may reflect group-membership or socio-cultural determinants in addition to personal determinants.

In conducting an informal analysis of the stories, I have found the following sequence to be helpful. Initially read through the story material and identify major story trends and themes. This should include an indication of the time frame of the stories (past, present, future) and the way in which the stories are resolved, i.e. positive, negative, incomplete. Following this, the stories can be examined in terms of their style and level of organization. Some questions to ask in this regard are: Do the stories appear to be mainly descriptive, symbolic or dramatic? To what extent do the plots appear logical and coherent? What level of creativity seems to be present? Is the language rich and expressive? and Do the stories appear detailed or is there a reliance on a more panoramic view? As a final task, the various characters in the stories should be considered. The heroes in the stories are of particular importance and should be assessed in terms of their motives, levels of personal agency (initiating or a pawn), feelings, and environmental presses (concerns) which come into play. A similar assessment of other characters can also prove interesting. Once the characters have been considered individually, the relationships between them can also be evaluated.

> *look for recurring themes; certain stories can be quite revealing and help develop some new personal insights.*

As with all projective methods, collaborative analysis is an essential element. With stories you will need to review all the material that has been generated with your client and look for recurring themes in it. Certain stories can be quite revealing and help develop some new personal insights.

The drawing tasks and story creations that have been presented thus far represent only the "tip of the iceberg" with respect to projective methods. Many other methods exist or can be developed by you. The starting point is an ambiguous stimulus and the request for a response to what has been presented. Stimulus situations have been created from post cards, sentence stems, poetry, sounds, photographs, and so on. The counselling process is, as usual, the most significant aspect of the method. What is important is an informal approach with active collaboration between the client and the counsellor.

Summary

The self-assessment activities that have been presented in the last two chapters are designed to act as a catalyst for self exploration with the goal being the acquisition of new perspectives on life problems. In presenting this series of activities, I am well aware that there are many other options which could be explored. What I have tried to do is to present some of the activities that I have personally found helpful; other theorists and counsellors might choose to elaborate other methods.

The next chapter continues the theme of problem resolution but moves beyond self-assessment to examine issues related to connecting with people and the labour market, decision making and preparation for job search.

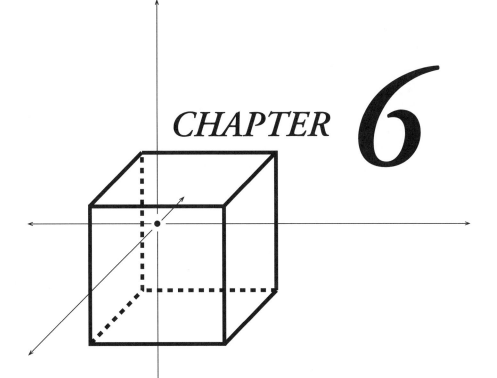

CHAPTER **6**

PROBLEM RESOLVING TASKS:

Connecting, Deciding, and Preparing

This chapter continues the emphasis upon problem-resolving tasks but shifts the attention from self-assessment to issues of connecting to the labour market and other people, decision making and preparing for job search. In many respects, the strategies presented here help to better define the "resolution pathway." As with the earlier material, an overview of a number of different practical strategies will be presented. The selection of the most appropriate strategy in any counselling situation depends on the particular needs of the client.

Labour Market Information

Many clients come to counselling seeking labour market information, often with the idea of focusing their efforts on the jobs with the best future prospects. While at one level this may appear to be a very laudable goal, it can often be a real problem for people, particularly when they are trying to pursue careers without taking into account their own personal suitability. On a number of occasions, I have met clients who wish to pursue "computers" without any regard to their interests or aptitudes. As I mentioned in Chapter Four, labour market information is only one piece of the "puzzle." Good career decision making depends on integrating labour market information with self awareness and a supportive context.

A. Labour Market Trends

Acquiring labour market information can occur at several different levels. At the broadest level, there is the identification of labour market trends. There are any number of books that can be consulted to focus attention on future trends. One of the most interesting books I have looked at recently was written by Reid (1996). As CEO of the Angus Reid polling group, Reid states that "the basic rules and patterns that made our lives predictable, that imposed a sense of order and continuity, no longer seem to apply" (p. 14). He identifies a number of rules that have previously served as guiding beacons but which now have begun to fade and are looking more like myths. Listed below are brief illustrations of some of these myths:

> *"basic rules and patterns that made our lives predictable, that imposed a sense of order and continuity, no longer seem to apply"*

1. Myth - Big is Safe

It used to be the case that security and safety could be found in size. If you were attached to a large organization, your job was secure. The government would be a good example of the ultimate form of security. For many people a job with the government was a "job for life." Today there is a growing recognition that there are no longer any safe areas. Most of the job growth has, in fact, taken place in the smaller companies.

2. Myth - Growth is Good for Everyone

With a rising stock market and a strong economy, we should see a reduction in unemployment and a spread of wealth throughout the nation. This just isn't happening! What is occurring is that much of the wealth is being funnelled into a few hands. To illustrate, consider that according to U.S. statistics (similar in Canada) corporate executives were making 44 times as much as workers in 1972, by 1992 the proportion had shifted to 222. Clearly the rich are getter richer and the gap between rich and poor is growing at an alarming pace.

3. Myth - Science and Technology Will Save Us

We certainly have been dazzled by scientific and technological advances. The current computer revolution is a good case in point. What we are now realizing, however, is that there are environmental and personal costs to many of the changes that have occurred. Science and technology are only tools, and as such the focus needs to be on the human values directing the development that is happening.

4. Myth - A Good Education Means a Good Job

While there is a clear connection between jobs and higher education, there is no longer the assurance that education will lead to work in the field in which one studied. As with the job market, there are no longer any safe fields of study and the relationship between education and work has become more complex.

5. Myth - Loyalty is All

Traditionally, loyalty to the company has been very high in the workplace. With downsizings and cutbacks, however, employees are increasingly having to become more self reliant. The psychological contract between employer and employee has been broken and loyalty in the workplace has suffered. Perhaps as a response to this change, there has been a desire for more loyalty from family and friends.

6. Myth - Location, Location, Location

The industrial revolution was characterized by a separation of work from the home. With the growth in telecommunications (cell phones, lap top computers, fax machines, e-mail, internet), however, and the high cost of real estate, many people are establishing alternate ways of working. These alternate arrangements reduce the dependence on physical proximity to a particular work site. Many people have the option of working from their homes with their main lines of contact with colleagues and customers being telecommunication linkages.

In this emerging labour market, people need to find their identity in new ways.

7. Myth - Time is Linear

Increasing globalization has brought us into a world where something is always happening somewhere. Our ability to rest and step outside of events has diminished. As a result there is a continuous sense of urgency as workers strive to cope with huge volumes of information. There never seems to be enough time to handle what needs to be done.

These myths and others have helped to define a very different type of working climate. In this emerging labour market, people need to find their identity in new ways. This new definition includes changes such as being open to life-long learning, defining oneself in terms of skills and achievements rather than job titles (a portfolio worker), piecing part-time and contract work together, learning how to market oneself in a competitive marketplace, thinking globally, and above all, being flexible (Herr, 1997). The first step toward acquiring this new perspective is an understanding of how the labour market has changed and is changing.

As clients look ahead to the future, you may find it helpful to have them focus on their overall impressions. One way of presenting an overall picture is by using metaphors and discussing change in the context of different metaphoric images. Gelatt (1991), in talking about the future, encourages people to look at the future by considering four different images. The first image is that of a "Roller Coaster" twisting through a fixed set of twists and turns in a dark setting. A second image is that of the "Mighty River" which pulls us along through quiet segments as well as periods of turmoil (rapids). The third image is that of the "Great Ocean" where we are navigating our way through the waters, wary of storms and other challenges. Lastly, there is the image of the "Colossal Dice Game" where things just happen by chance and we hope for good luck. There are undoubtedly other images that could be applied, and it is interesting to look at the images that we have of the future as well as those of our clients. The point of this exercise is to help people to identify their personal images of the future.

B. The Internet and Other Resources

The Internet can be an excellent source of information on labour market options. There are many different sites which offer the user an opportunity to browse through descriptions of various jobs. A good place to start in Canada is with the Job Futures web site (http://www.hrdc-drhc.gc.ca/hrdc/corp/stratpol/jobs/english/index.html). This site provides an alphabetical listing of jobs, as well as a more focused listing using the following broad skill types:

- Business, Finance and Administration Occupations

- Natural and Applied Sciences and Related Occupations

- Health Occupations

- Occupations in Social Science, Education, Government Service and Religion

- Occupations in Art, Culture, Recreation and Sport

- Sales and Service Occupations

- Trades, Transport and Equipment Operators and Related Occupations

- Occupations Unique to Primary Industry

- Occupations Unique to Processing, Manufacturing and Utilities

Other sites that are worth visiting as part of a general exploration for information include the following:

- Occupational Outlook Handbook

  (http://stats.bls.gov/ocohome.htm)

  This site was developed by the U.S. government and not only provides information on specific occupations but also discusses occupations of the future.

- Career Considerations, Human Resources Development Canada

  (http://www.globalx.net/ocd/career/car-eng/index.html)

  This site was developed by the Canadian federal government and lists occupations according to 19 occupational groups and provides examples of occupations under each.

- Making Career Sense of Labour Market Information

  (http://www.ceiss.org/randa/making/mcstoc.htm)

- Labour Market Information, Human Resources Development Canada

  (http:/www.hrdc-drhc.gc.ca/common/lmi.shtml)

- Canada WorkInfoNet

  (http://www.workinfonet.ca)

- Work Futures

  (http://workinfonet.bc.ca/WorkFutures)

- The Strategis site from Industry Canada

  (http://strategis.ic.gc.ca/engdoc/main.html)

While the internet is obviously a tremendous resource for occupational information, it is not the only way to acquire information. Clients need to also consider community resources such as:

- local libraries - most libraries have career sections which contain a wide variety of resources; computer access to the internet is also often possible.

- yellow pages - the telephone book can be a great source of information about local community organizations.

- community centers - they often offer career-related programs.

- career centers; both private and government career counselling programs often have relevant programs and resource centers.

- schools (high schools, colleges, universities) - programs and information.

These resources can help stimulate ideas about occupational options.

Learning to read and interpret information beyond the help wanted sections of the newspaper is also something that you may want to focus on with clients. For instance, suppose that a client reads that a new large factory is going to be locating in a community. There certainly will be some jobs related to the specific industry, but there may also be some other spin-offs. Other businesses may benefit from the incoming factory and increase their hiring accordingly. The prudent job seeker is often one who can anticipate these possibilities and connect with employers in these other related industries before the hiring advertisements appear in the newspapers (if, in fact, they ever do). Teaching clients to look not only at the present, but also at future possibilities is an important career exploration skill.

C. Expanding Labour Market Options

The process of discovering different labour market options need not stop with the identification of a particularly interesting occupation. In some respects this is only the beginning. Once an occupation of interest has been identified, it is helpful to explore some of the related occupational possibilities. This exploration can take many forms. In the Career Pathways program (Amundson & Poehnell, 1996) there is an exercise where clients start with a specific occupation and then brainstorm other related occupations. The end result of this process is a career expansion diagram such as the one in Figure Ten:

Figure Ten: Career Expansion

Using this approach, you will be able to combine brainstorming with an interesting visual presentation. This process of expansion helps to extend the viewpoint through which clients look at occupations.

Another way to help people expand their options is to challenge them with the possibility of starting their own businesses. For many people, "jobs" are only to be "found," and they never entertain the possibility of creating their own work. Becoming an entrepreneur is, of course, not for everyone, but it is an important avenue to explore. Research on entrepreneurial behaviour (Bird, 1989) has indicated that the following personal characteristics are associated with successful entrepreneurs: focus on achievement, relate well with others, self confident, flexible, organized, adventuresome, high energy, risk-taking, hard-working, optimistic, independent, persistent, and open-minded. From my observations, I have noted that there seem to be many different pathways into the entrepreneurial mode. For some people, it is all they ever wanted to do in life and they wouldn't have it any other way. Others, however, are not similarly inclined but realize that it is the best option given their life circumstances. With this latter group, it is important that they receive assistance with both the planning and implementation process. With encouragement and some practical assistance, they often can be very successful entrepreneurs.

Support and Informational Networking

When people are involved in the career exploration process at whatever level, they need input and encouragement from others. One illustration of a formal network comes from Burton and Wedemeyer (1991), facilitators of a Career Management Seminar in New York through the Harvard Business School. They indicate that people seeking a career change often feel out of control and powerless in the face of many challenges. To counteract this perspective, they suggest that people view themselves as the CEO of a corporation. In this instance, they are the CEO in charge of their job search and, as such, have the following functions and responsibilities:

- to assess their strengths and weaknesses;

- to propose and direct a carefully devised job search strategy based on their initial assessment; and

- to reach those elements in the market place where their strengths are most well suited and to limit liabilities.

Most corporations have a Board of Directors and the same would apply in this scenario. The members on the Board are there to provide input, to act as a "sounding board" for new ideas, and to provide support and encouragement. Burton and Wedemeyer suggest that the Board include about ten persons. Some factors to consider when choosing Board members would be: availability, positive attitude, good judgment, honesty and integrity, open-

One of the greatest dangers in the career transition process comes from the isolation associated with looking for work.

mindedness, and knowledge of the field (education and working life). Meetings with various Board members would occur on a regular basis (probably not with all of them at the same time, although this would be a possibility); and at these meetings, the focus would be on discussing the current situation and setting directions for future activities. With this type of arrangement, there would be great opportunities for informational and emotional support.

Even if clients do not choose to formally set up a Board of Directors, there is considerable advantage in having them informally dialogue with friends and family members on a regular basis. One of the greatest dangers in the career transition process comes from the isolation associated with looking for work (Amundson & Borgen, 1987). Maintaining contact with others is a good coping strategy for both emotional and practical well being. To ensure that connections are made and maintained, you may want to encourage your clients to become part of a career exploration or job search support group. In this way, there are opportunities to extend contacts by regularly meeting with others who are involved in a similar exploration or job search process.

When you consider the advantages of support groups, remember that the advantages come not only from being helped by others but also from offering a helping hand. I still remember the first career exploration / job search group that I ran. In the beginning, each person had the opportunity to briefly tell their story. The first woman described how she had moved here with her husband and daughter looking for work. On the way there was a truck accident and they lost most of their possessions. They had a difficult time finding work after arriving and this put a strain on the family; this, in turn, led to a marital separation. She was able to find a job in the northern part of the province and left to work in a small community. While there, her daughter was raped and she decided to return with her daughter to Vancouver. And now, she found herself in this group that I was leading. Naturally, there were considerable tears in the telling of the story and the atmosphere in the room was tense. The next person to tell their story was an older man who had worked all his life as a labourer. The factory where he had been working had shut down and he couldn't find work. He talked about competing for jobs with eighteen year olds. Despite his experience, he was not getting even the most basic jobs. As before, the tears also started to flow; and the woman reached out to him and gave him a hug. At that moment I understood experientially the power of the group. My role as a counsellor was to facilitate the process, but much of the helping came from other group members as they reached out emotionally and in other practical ways to help one another.

Another aspect of networking involves teaching clients how to connect with others about information related to their occupational interests. The informational interview is one way in which clients approach others to learn more about working life. From my experience, the best source of information often comes from people working in the field, and they usually are quite willing to share their time and expertise. In arranging these interviews, I find it important to stress to clients the purpose of the interviews. The idea is to get information and, thus, it should not be confused with a job interview. The focus here is upon learning more about a particular occupation by talking with someone who is working in that area. Clients coming to these interviews should be prepared and have a list of questions that they would like to pursue. The interviews should probably last no longer than about 20 minutes unless there is a clear indication that time is not a factor. The questions generally focus on how the person got into their position (education, work experiences, etc.), what their duties are in the job, how the job has changed over time, what their likes and dislikes are, and what the prospects are for the future. As a concluding question, it is often helpful to enquire about anyone else that they would recommend for an interview. For each interview, clients should keep detailed notes and send thank you cards.

Many people are too private with their problems and as a result miss golden opportunities. I have become a real believer in serendipity over the years.

In addition to formal networking activities, there is also a place for informal networking with friends and neighbours who are working in completely unrelated areas. Many people are too private with their problems and as a result miss golden opportunities. I have become a real believer in serendipity over the years. There are so many occasions when chance occurrences lead to great connections. As an illustration of the power of informal networks, I remember the time when myself and a colleague were working with some counsellor trainers in Hungary. They were coming to Canada for an official visit and the challenge for us was to find Hungarian interpreters. I was completely at a loss as to how we would ever accomplish this task. I didn't know anyone who spoke Hungarian and couldn't find anything in the telephone directory. At a meeting with a group of friends, I shared my problem and another fellow indicated that he knew someone who would be perfect for the job. After telling a few people about my need, I was able to develop a long list of potential candidates, all ready to do the job just for the experience. A second interpreter from another city was located using official channels. The advantages of the informal network translated into considerable savings and a unique experience. In job search groups, people often make interesting connections with others who are working in totally different areas. There always seems to be someone who has a neighbour or a friend who could offer assistance.

Involving Significant Others
in the Counselling

One of the counselling conventions that was mentioned in Chapter Two was that most career counselling occurs with an individual focus with few connections to the broader social community. The viewpoints of family members and/or friends may be discussed, but there is usually no attempt to bring them directly into the counselling process. This individual focus is a reflection of our individualistic society and the belief that people need to have the freedom to make their career choices without influence from either family or friends.

> *There are many situations where the opinions of others are important for the career decision making that is underway.*

While this may sound good in theory, there are many cultural groups with more group-oriented values. There are also many situations where the opinions of others are important for the career decision making that is underway. For example, many young people are dependent on their parents for emotional and material support and are comfortable discussing career issues together. With married adults, there are many dual career families where the decisions that are being made must be made together. Certainly there are a number of instances where some direct involvement would be helpful.

Often, when we talk about involving others in career counselling, there is the assumption that all members will be taking an equal role in the process, similar to a family counselling session. I have discovered, mostly by "trial and error," that it often works best to involve others in primarily an observational capacity. That is there is a clear distinction between the person being counselled and others who come to the session as guests of the client. The visitors are invited to participate in the process as observers and within this capacity, they have some opportunities to provide input at regularly scheduled intervals.

An article by Amundson and Penner (1998) illustrates how the above procedure can be applied when working with young people and their parents. With this approach, two or three young people are invited to a career counselling session along with at least one of their parents. The focus in these sessions is on the career needs and perspectives of the young people, with an opportunity for input by their parents throughout the course of the counselling sessions. During these sessions, parents have the opportunity to share their perspective on the labour market and also to comment on how they view their children, i.e. skills, interests, aptitudes, personality, values. Most important, however, is the fact that they spend some of the time in an observational role listening to what is being said. This type of scenario obviously depends on having the foundation of a positive relationship between parents and their children.

Another counselling situation where direct involvement of significant others has been tried is within the First Nations communities. A recent article by McCormick and Amundson (1997) describes a counselling approach where family and community members are invited to career counselling sessions. These sessions are characterized by some unique qualities, i.e. prayer, ceremonies, the talking stick or eagle feather. The involvement of significant others is determined through access to the talking stick. The overall process is designed to help each person "publicly state their roles and responsibilities and to help the client to feel supported by their family and community" (p. 178).

Direct involvement of significant others is not always possible; and in many instances, it is sufficient to have friends and family members contribute information through a questionnaire (Amundson, 1984). Listed below is an illustration of a questionnaire that is used as part of the Starting Points program (Westwood, Amundson, Borgen, Bailey & Davies, 1994).

Significant Other Questionnaire

Please complete the following questions. Your opinion is important to help _____ make future career plans; therefore, your honesty is greatly appreciated.

1. What would you say this person is good at? What skills has this person demonstrated?

2. What would you see as this person's major interest areas?

3. How would you describe the personal characteristics of this person?

4. What positive changes have you noticed over time in this person, especially in relation to work or looking for work?

5. In what ways could this person continue to improve?

6. If you were to suggest the ideal job or career prospects for this person, what would it be?

In using this questionnaire, you will need to spend some initial time discussing with clients who should be asked to contribute information. There also should be time afterwards for debriefing the information.

Decision Making Strategies

At some point in the career exploration process, clients are faced with the task of assessing the viability of various options. Certain decision making strategies can be employed at these points to help clients move forward with their career planning.

The starting point in many cases is to pinpoint what actually needs to be decided. When working with adolescent clients, I am often confronted by their desire to map out the rest of their lives, or failing that, at least a full college/ university program of studies. What many of them fail to recognize is the fact that in many instances they only

> *Decision making is a process and there are times when you don't need to have everything "worked out" in order to move forward.*

need to figure out the first step. Decision making is a process and there are times when you don't need to have everything "worked out" in order to move forward. For example, they may need to decide whether they are going to a college or university and, if so, what general program they will take in their first year; but beyond that, they can keep their options open. Learning to assess what actually needs to be decided is an important first step, and in general the operating rule is to keep as many options open as possible with the choices that are being made.

A.   Cognitive Decision Making Methods

One of the most common cognitive decision making methods is to have clients make a simple list of the advantages and disadvantages of adopting various stances. Putting the information down on paper often allows a fresh perspective on the problem. Discussing the list with another person also may help to clarify difficult situations.

Another way to assess situations is to use the Wheel (Amundson and Poehnell, 1996) as a way to check various options. With this method, a particular career choice is placed in the centre of the Wheel and then each segment of the Wheel is examined to determine how it fits with the particular career choice that is being highlighted. If, for example, a client was considering nursing as a career, the career would be examined in terms of its fit with the person's unique combination of skills, interests, values, personality, and general work and educational background. Support from significant others would also be considered along with labour market possibilities. Gati (1986) has used the term "sequential elimination method" to describe this approach. The basic idea is that you start with the desired occupational choice, and then examine it fully (using the various factors identified in the Wheel) before examining other possibilities.

> *Putting the information*
> *down on paper*
> *often allows*
> *a fresh perspective*
> *on the problem.*

There are times when more than one option seems viable; and under these conditions, a repertory grid method of decision making can be effective. The repertory grid starts by having clients identify ten of the major considerations (values) they use to assess occupational options. You then ask them to list several of the specific occupational options they are considering and use the considerations (values) as a framework for making an assessment. By using the person's unique combination of considerations, you can assess several options at the same time using a grid framework. To illustrate this process, consider the grid (Figure Eleven) which has been used as an illustration in the Career Pathways program (Amundson and Poehnell, 1996, p. 62).

In this example the Employment Counsellor choice is ranked highest overall and in most of the categories. The only place where the Social Worker option received a higher rating was in "helping others."

Figure Eleven: Decision Making Grid

(Factors)	(Career Options) 1. Social Worker	2. Employment Counsellor	3. Counsellor in a Group Home	4. Financial Assistance Worker
1. Challenge	+5	+5	+3	+2
2. Freedom	+4	+4	+3	+1
3. Flexibility	+4	+4	+2	+1
4. Use Abilities	+2	+4	+1	0
5. Exciting	+2	+3	+1	0
6. Creativity	+2	+4	+1	0
7. Money	+3	+4	+2	+2
8. Reward Hard Work	+2	+2	+1	0
9. Help Others	+4	+3	+2	+1
10. Opportunity to Travel	0	0	+1	0
Total Score	28	33	16	7

The advantage of using a grid system for analysis is that it is very concrete and the information is displayed in an interesting manner. In working with grids, you will need to consider a number of issues. Perhaps the most basic is whether the ratings that are made reflect reality. Using the example mentioned above, is it true that an employment counsellor position allows you to express your creativity? This is something which might be checked by going through an informational interview. Thus, one of your tasks is to help clients conduct reality checks of the ratings that are being made. Discussing the relative merits of the various options using a specific factor can also be an important task to consider. Clients may have certain boundaries beyond which they are not willing to compromise. For example, wages may need to be at a certain level and anything lower is just unacceptable. Thus, even if everything else is rated highly, the category of wages functions as a determining factor. A work position with a lower rating may be more acceptable because of the higher wages. Of course, the most obvious factor to discuss with this method is the relative scores of the various options. There usually are "winners" and "losers," but sometimes the differences in scores are insufficient to separate the options. This is a general form of assessment and the scores must be interpreted accordingly.

B. Intuitive Decision Making

For many clients, decision making is more than just a consideration of various factors; it reaches down to their "soul" and is very intuitive. "Feeling right" about a decision can be the most critical factor in the decision making process. The intuitive perspective can be facilitated through a number of activities. The starting point is usually the development of the right atmosphere, one of peace and tranquility rather than busyness and stress. Barbara Moses (1997) makes the following statement when describing what happens to us when we start to find ourselves overextended and just too busy:

> When we fall into this frenzy of busyness, we start to function on "automatic" We don't think about what we are doing. We just *do* it. There is no time to *experience* the experience. We are too busy just reacting. Under such pressures, everything is flat, and there are no highlights or lows. There is no lustre. We are on autopilot. Still less do we have time to reflect about why we are working so hard. We just work. And the harder we work, and the busier we make ourselves, the less time we have to examine the way we are living. (pp. 80, 81)

Moving outside of the busyness can be facilitated through relaxation, physical exercises, walks in nature, meditation, prayer, imagination, and so on. Encouraging clients to take time for themselves is usually a good way to locate the right frame of mind.

Allowing for an incubation period is often good advice when clients are facing a difficult decision. Sometimes the best way to deal with an impasse is to have clients step away from the problem, do something else, let the unconscious take over. Coming back to the problem after a period of rest/ change often produces new perspectives and an increased likelihood of making good decisions.

> *"Feeling right" about a decision can be the most critical factor in the decision making process.*

Viewing problems from the vantage point of peace and tranquility helps clients to engage the problem in a more holistic manner, taking account of the complexities without being overwhelmed. Within this frame of mind, they can be more imaginative and also be more aware of their personal needs at many different levels, i.e. emotional, physical, mental, spiritual.

Richard Foster (1978), when talking about the pathways to spiritual growth, frames his discussion using the term "disciplines." These disciplines can have an inward focus (meditation, prayer, fasting, study), an outward focus (simplicity, solitude, submission, service), and also a corporate emphasis (confession, worship, guidance, celebration). His point is that there are things that we can do to facilitate the content for personal reflection.

Paradoxical Solutions

A. Positive Uncertainty

The dichotomy between cognitive and intuitive decision making has been challenged in recent years by the former cognitive (rational) theorist, H.B. Gelatt (1989, 1991). He is notable in that in recent years he has changed his mind and now finds the rational model to be insufficient in the face of current challenges. The following quotation from the preface of his book on creative decision making outlines what he now considers to be the most functional approach:

> What is needed now is balance. Today everything is changing so fast that it isn't wise to rely only on old formulas, standard practices, and limited models for deciding what to do. A balance must be found between always deciding by strict adherence to a scientific formula and always deciding by instinct. It isn't an improvement to be totally ruled by intuition over being totally ruled by logic... We need some decision advice that is more closely related to what people do than to what experts say they should do. In this book I'm saying, *Have a logical process for making decisions and use something else. That is advice, and it is custom.* However, the something else I'm advocating is positive uncertainty. Positive uncertainty is a balanced, versatile, whole-brain decision strategy featuring the creative tools of flexibility, optimism, and imagination. (p. i)

The notion of positive uncertainty is interesting in that two seemingly opposite ideas are being held together within the same concept. Gelatt is asking people to be positive about what they are doing and at the same time maintaining a healthy degree of wariness and uncertainty. He is suggesting that we move from "either/or" to "both/and" thinking.

In today's labour market, it is easy to see how some paradoxical concepts might help make sense of the situation. At the same time as employers are calling for loyalty and productivity, they are often creating unstable working environments where uncertainty is the norm. To cope with this type of environment, people need to recognize the uncertainty but, at the same time, proceed with clear direction. People who cannot handle the paradoxical elements within the situation find themselves in a difficult situation. If they are positive without any uncertainty, they may not give themselves the protection they need. If they are consumed by uncertainty, they may find themselves paralyzed and ineffective.

> *Positive uncertainty is a balanced, versatile, whole-brain decision strategy featuring the creative tools of flexibility, optimism, and imagination.*

Gelatt (1991, p. 12) proposes four paradoxical principles which help to define positive uncertainty. These principles are listed below along with a brief description of each:

1. Be focused and flexible about what you want

    - Know what you want but don't be sure

    - Treat goals as hypotheses

    - Balance achieving goals with discovering them

2. Be aware and wary about what you know

    - Recognize that knowledge is power and ignorance is bliss

- Treat memory as an enemy

- Balance using information with imagination

3. Be objective and optimistic about what you believe

  - Notice that reality is in the eye and the I of the beholder

  - Treat beliefs as prophecy

  - Balance reality testing with wishful-thinking

4. Be practical and magical about what you do

  - Learn to plan and plan to learn

  - Treat intuition as real

  - Balance responding to change with causing change

It is clear from reviewing these ideas that imagination, creativity and intuition play a key role in the decision making process that Gelatt is suggesting in these principles.

You can use the concept of positive uncertainty to help clients realize that there might be some creative solutions to the barriers they are facing. Sometimes all that is required is a reconceptualization which allows clients to "draw outside the lines." As an illustration, consider the dilemma of a young man trying to decide whether to go into teaching or woodwork. One possible solution is to become a woodwork teacher. Another option is to follow one direction for paid work but keep up involvements outside of work in the other area (coaching teams, joining a wood carving club, getting involved in set design at the local theatre, and so on). With this perspective it is often possible to "have your cake and eat it too."

I have found the positive uncertainty concept particularly helpful when working with clients who want to set long term goals. Students coming to the end of high school often are anxious because they cannot definitively set a clear long-term goal. Certainly the desire for certainty is understandable, but in today's labour market it is advisable to hold the future "with more of an open hand." In most cases all that really needs to be decided upon is the first step. Students planning to go to university may need to decide between arts or science, but further decision making can wait until later.

> *Sometimes all that is required is a reconceptualization which allows clients to "draw outside the lines."*

B.   The "S" Curve

Another theorist, Charles Handy (1994), a renowned organizational analyst from Great Britain, makes the point that we can characterize many of life's transitions using an "S" curve. That is, at the start there are always some challenges and this is the dip at the bottom of the S. After this initial adjustment period there is a strong upward movement. But upward movement does not carry on forever and at some point there is a plateauing and eventually a decline. The unknown features of this pattern is the length of time that is spent in any one position.

Handy makes the point that we need to learn how to "slide off" the S as it reaches its peak, and catch another S for new movement upwards. The difficulty comes with the fact that most of us want to get off the curve only after a clear downwards movement is detected. By the time the "tide has turned," it is often too late and we end up following the downward slide to the bottom. The paradoxical element in this perspective is that we are being called to make changes when things are going well. Incidentally, anyone who has ever played the stock market knows the reality of the S-curve. All too often, stock market players watch excitedly as their stock climbs to great heights and then stay watching as the bottom drops out.

With Handy's model, there are two mistakes that one can make. On the one hand you can jump off too early and lose the strong upward movement that will continue for a period of time. Or you can hang on for too long and lose the opportunity to move over to a more positive situation. The dilemma is not an easy one to resolve.

The dilemma that Handy poses seems particularly relevant given the current labour market. Growing numbers of workers find themselves hanging on to jobs that have a limited time span or find themselves creating products with a limited run. As contract workers, consultants, portfolio workers, entrepreneurs or even workers in standard jobs, they may be doing well at the moment but are unsure about how long everything will last. Living with this constant tension can take its toll on family and personal life.

The paradoxical element in this perspective is that we are being called to make changes when things are going well.

One of the ways to "step outside the lines" with this particular problem is to begin preparing oneself for an exit while still firmly attached to the task at hand. Describing this movement in colloquial terms, one might say that you "shouldn't put all your eggs in one basket." It is important through active networking to keep aware of other openings and new projects that might be feasible. Positioning for new opportunities is another strategy that can be worthwhile. Some people position themselves by acquiring additional training and experiences that they can use to good advantage when opportunities arise. Take, for example, one young man who wanted to get into insurance underwriting. While working as a clerk at the insurance company, he took some evening courses to prepare himself for future opportunities. After a few tries, he was able to get a position based on his educational training and also his networking within the company.

Another way to conceptualize this issue is by using the metaphor of motion and movement. It takes a lot more energy to get yourself going if you are standing still! Anyone who has played sports knows that the person in a stationary position is much more vulnerable that the one who is in motion. Maintaining career momentum is essential in today's turbulent labour market. While you are working at a particular task, it is important to maintain a certain career momentum. Having worked with many unemployed people, I find that one of the saddest commentaries is the statement, "*I just didn't see it coming and when it hit it was too late—we were all scrambling for the few remaining jobs.*"

Behavioural Rehearsal Strategies

As clients move forward with their job search, they may find themselves in need of some additional learning (one of the employment dimensions). They may lack the skills to contact potential employers or to handle themselves in interviews. One of the strategies that can be particularly helpful at this point is behavioural rehearsal training–this will be familiar territory for people familiar with the Azrin, Flores and Kaplan (1975) Job Club.

Your role, when you are using behavioural rehearsal strategies, becomes one of being a "coach" or "guide." You need to have specific knowledge and know how to take complex tasks and break them down into manageable units for learning. Perhaps most important, you need to know how to give encouragement and how to provide constructive positive feedback to clients.

There are certain specific steps in the behavioural rehearsal process. Westwood (1994) has developed the following twelve-step behavioural rehearsal sequence that can be applied in a number of different domains:

1. **Assess:** use basic observation and communication skills to determine what specifically needs to be learned.

2. **Explain:** describe the background of what is going to be addressed using specific examples.

3. **Preliminary Modelling:** demonstrate the specific skill(s) through role playing.

4. **Comment & Question:** encourage clients to discuss what they saw and heard and clarify any areas of confusion.

5. **Initial Practice:** invite clients to try to repeat/simulate what was previously modelled.

6. **Feedback & Encouragement:** focus on the positive achievements and add correction where necessary.

> *Your role becomes one of being a "coach" or "guide." Assuming this role necessitates that you have specific knowledge about what needs to be learned.*

7. **Repeat Modelling (when necessary):** show clients a second time by doing another role playing demonstration.

8. **Comments & Questions:** repeat as above with clients discussing how to incorporate additional changes, i.e. fine tuning.

9. **Additional Practice:** repeat step number five.

10. **Feedback & Encouragement:** repeat step number six.

11. **Goal Setting & Contracting:** encourage clients to practice their skill(s) in actual situations. Allow time for additional practice as is necessary.

12. **Follow-Up:** check on progress and provide additional encouragement and practice.

Westwood's comprehensive behavioural rehearsal strategy is designed to provide ample opportunity for instruction, demonstration, practice, encouragement and correction. Depending on the complexity of the behaviours to be learned, you may find it necessary to repeat the process several times focusing on different learning tasks.

The various role-playing demonstrations and actions that have been described by Westwood can by enhanced by using audio/video recording and playback (as mentioned in the previous chapter). By incorporating this strategy into your counselling, you will have the opportunity with clients to focus on specific behavioural actions, to pinpoint problems, and to highlight successes.

The practice component within a behavioural rehearsal strategy can also be expanded by using the concept of visualization . With visualization, clients practise situations in their minds by focusing on each step of the process and by imagining themselves successfully completing tasks. This element of visualization can be an important addition to the standard behavioural rehearsal process.

Summary

The practical strategies that have been described in this chapter emphasize three key elements: (a) preparing - information acquisition (instructional and coached practice), (b) connecting - support from others, and (c) deciding - cognitive, intuitive, and paradoxical decision making. Through involvement in these type of activities, clients acquire the practical information and skills that they need to resolve problems.

This concludes the chapters focusing on problem resolving tasks. The next chapter shifts to issues of closure and outlines some of the tasks that can be effectively used during this last phase of the counselling process.

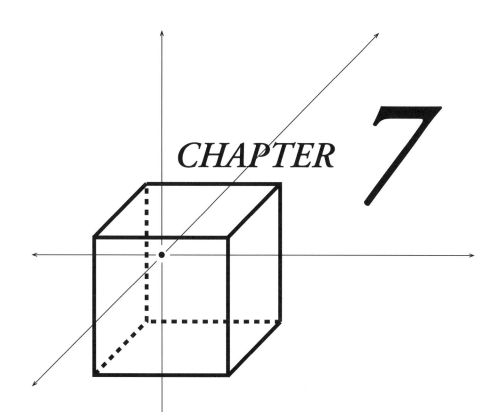

CHAPTER 7

PROBLEM CLOSING TASKS

This final segment of the counselling process brings to a close the exchange between counsellors and clients. As you reach this closure, there is the hope and expectation that some movement has been made toward resolving the problem(s) that have been presented. At this juncture, I very much appreciate the wisdom of the brief and solution-focused counsellors who celebrate the gains that have been achieved but also realize that clients may need to do more work at some future time. Most career counsellors operate within a limited time frame; thus, the closing tasks are dictated by what can be achieved within a prescribed time period.

The decision to end the counselling involvement certainly is affected strongly by practical realities, but there is also something to be negotiated between counsellor and client. There seems to be a point at which there is some form of mutual agreement about the time for ending. The signal about closure can come from either person and is often as much a non-verbal as a verbal statement. Once the issue of closure is recognized by both parties, the negotiation can begin. Clients may request more time to work on other issues, and counsellors may also indicate that other things need to be done to ensure a satisfactory ending. Either party can end the counselling relationship, but there is little doubt that the best outcomes are the result of mutual agreement.

In ending the counselling relationship, I believe that it is important to regard the period of closure as a separate aspect of counselling with its own special qualities and time requirements. Many counsellors make the mistake of rushing through the ending process without enough regard for due process. Speaking openly about the upcoming ending and giving advance notice are important tasks in bringing about successful closure. Some situations do lend themselves to a relatively quick ending; but, even then, there is a need to devote some time to the closure phase.

Summarizing the
Counselling Process

Once a decision for closure has been articulated, counsellors and clients can begin to reflect upon what has been accomplished in the time that they have been together. These reflections go back to the original statement of the problem and continue through to the various resolving tasks that were employed. During this reflective process, you have the opportunity to identify and comment upon some of the client strengths that you observed.

> *I have found it important to highlight particular "moments of movement" ... points in the counselling process where there seemed to be clear indicators of a change in perspective.*

A form of interpersonal recall can be used to review what has transpired during the counselling sessions. With this approach, the starting point is always the recollections of clients. As counsellors, we have ideas about what worked and what didn't, and it is interesting to step outside our personal framework and let clients tell us how they perceived the process. Differences in perspective are common and serve as an important feedback mechanism.

In reviewing the various aspects of counselling, I have found it important to highlight particular "moments of movement." These moments are points in the counselling process where there seemed to be clear indicators of a change in perspective (reframing). During these incidents, clients typically respond with comments such as the following:

> *"That really has got me thinking. I never looked at it that way before."*

> *"I used to feel really down when people wouldn't take my resume. Now when I get turned down, I try to learn from it and develop new ways to make my presentation."*

By focusing on these special moments, you help to consolidate the learning and movement that occurred during the counselling sessions.

The recollection of events is, of course, only one part of the summary process. The other element which is of critical importance is the description of positive personal attributes which have been observed. It is particularly helpful here to identify any changes which might have been noted. A statement such as the following incorporates this strength challenge perspective:

> *"When you now talk about your goals it is evident that you have a real sense of purpose. At the start you indicated that everything was confusing, but you've really worked hard to find your way to the place where you are today."*

Setting aside time for the summary provides both you and your clients with a specified time period for reviewing what has been accomplished through the counselling process. This review supports the changes that have been made and serves as a stepping stone for further action planning.

Acknowledging Feelings of Loss and Uncertainty

The strength of the interpersonal bond between counsellors and clients is often used to further counselling goals. Clients who form a close working alliance with their counsellors are more likely to have a successful counselling experience (Gelso & Carter, 1985). The positive interpersonal conditions for successful counselling, however, also make it more difficult to disengage (for both clients and counsellors). Feelings of loss are a common occurrence during the termination phase and need to be acknowledged as such. At the start of this book, I mentioned that many counsellors and clients have difficulties with beginnings and endings, the bookends of counselling. The experience of loss is certainly a very real factor in many counselling relationships.

> *Preparing for termination starts right at the beginning of counselling.*

Preparing for termination starts right at the beginning of counselling. As you set the initial goals, there often is some discussion about how long the counselling will continue. Setting a target date helps to frame counselling in such a way that there are some expectations with regard to closure. In a situation with multiple sessions, it can be helpful to bring up the topic of ending several weeks before the actual closing session. A comment such as the following is appropriate during this period:

> *"We are certainly making some good progress here. It is hard to believe how fast time is going. In another two weeks (assuming weekly sessions) we will have reached our goal."*

The point in making these comments is to reinforce the positive change that is being made and to draw attention to the impending conclusion of counselling sessions.

During the final counselling session, it is quite appropriate for you to mention feelings of loss. Often this type of discussion is best initiated by a self-disclosure statement. A statement such as the following is common in this situation:

> *"I am really going to miss our weekly sessions. I have enjoyed getting to know you and admire your courage and persistence in your career search."*

Of course, not every situation is going to result in feelings of loss, and counsellors are well advised to comment only in those instances where there are genuine feelings.

Another common emotion which characterizes the conclusion of counselling is that of uncertainty. Through counselling, many clients find themselves building their self esteem and energy levels. There is a natural fear that once the counselling "props" have been removed, everything will fall apart. This is really where self-management skills come into prominence. You need to be able to assure clients that they in fact do have the skills to be successful on their own. Pinpointing specific examples of competence lends credibility to statements of assurance.

In situations where clients are having difficulty dealing with loss or uncertainty, it is not uncommon for them to make requests to extend the counselling sessions. At this point, it is important that you distinguish between legitimate requests and situations where there is really little to be gained through continued contact. When you are dealing with requests for extensions, you may find if helpful to have in place the possibility of drop-in contacts and follow-up.

Developing an Action Plan

Action planning is a very significant part of bringing closure to the counselling process. Through development of the action plan, there is an opportunity to consolidate learning and to launch clients toward new phases of self-initiated action. It would be misleading, however, to suggest that all clients leave counselling with complete resolution of their problems. For many, counselling is merely one step in a lengthy journey.

It is helpful when thinking of action planning to look at goal setting with respect to both short- and long-term action planning. To help your clients deal with difficult situations, you may want to focus their attention on concrete and attainable goals. The assumption here is that through making some small changes, the larger picture will also be affected. Walter and Peller (1992) offer the following suggestions about how to frame goals so that there is a higher likelihood of success:

> *The assumption here is that through making some small changes, the larger picture will also be affected.*

- Be positive when stating goals. Emphasize what will be accomplished through the action plan.

- Use action words (e.g.. verbs ending with "ing": researching, writing, calling) to describe intentions.

- Focus on the present. What is going to happen after the client leaves the counselling session?

- Be specific and think through all details.

- Pay particular attention to those areas that are within the client's personal control.

- Use examples and metaphors which are within the client's experience and understanding.

These suggestions are designed to point clients toward concrete and realistic activities that have a high likelihood of success.

In order for action planning to be effective, it is imperative that clients feel some ownership over the plans that are being developed. Without this client involvement, there is every likelihood that little will happen following the counselling sessions. At this stage you need to be particularly careful that you have full client participation and support for what is being suggested.

Counsellors play an important role during this phase in helping clients to specify exactly what is going to happen next. It is not enough to know that the next step is to contact the college to get information about upcoming programs. In addition, clients need to specify when they will be making the call and who they will be calling. Challenging clients to think through all the details is an essential component of action planning.

In addition to specifying details of the action plan, you may also need to check to see that your clients have back-up plans in the event that things do not work out as they had anticipated. Many clients have one plan of action and falter when confronted by unexpected obstacles. In today's labour market, there are any number of uncertainties and clients need to be prepared to operate in this new reality. Anticipating potential obstacles boosts confidence and increases the general level of preparedness. You can help your clients by brainstorming and practising responses to difficult situations.

The consolidation of the action planning process comes when clients are able to put on paper, in their own words, what they will be doing in the short term and in the long term. Writing out the plan helps to make it more concrete and it becomes something for which they are accountable. While not legally binding, having the plan on paper acts as a form of contract between client and counsellor. Both persons then sign the document to acknowledge the

a case can be made for considering action planning as an integral part of every aspect of counselling

seriousness of the intent. The "ceremonial" signing of the plan reinforces at a symbolic level a client's commitment to following through with the appropriate action. As a further reinforcement, you may want to contact clients at a later date to check on the viability of the plan and what has been accomplished. This personal expression of interest serves as a motivator and often is enough to re-engage clients in their action planning. Follow-up is also an effective means of gathering data with respect to the effectiveness of the counselling that was undertaken. At another level, the action plans can simply be mailed to clients approximately one month after they have been completed. Little has to be said about the plans; just receiving them in the mail reminds clients of the commitments they made earlier.

A special case of action planning occurs when you decide to move directly from problem identification to closure, and find yourself looking for ways to make appropriate referrals. Under these circumstances, your role becomes that of a consultant. The main task is the placement of clients in appropriate counselling or educational programs. In these circumstances you need to have a good understanding of existing programs and personnel. Your professional judgment is relied upon when clients are considering other resources. One aspect of professional judgment is your self knowledge about the limits of your expertise. Without this self knowledge, you may find yourself "in over your head" and in desperate need of other consultations.

While the role of action planning has been closely tied to the closure phase of counselling, a case can be made for considering action planning as an integral part of every aspect of counselling. The very act of coming for counselling is a form of action planning. Clients consider their options and for whatever reasons choose to enter into a counselling relationship (assuming voluntary participation). In many situations, the presenting problems change shape as the discussion proceeds. Some of these changes are the result of attaining a better understanding of the counselling process; other changes are the result of developing a trusting relationship with the counsellor. I believe that it is important to be ever vigilant with respect to the changing needs of clients and to be prepared to address these changes as they occur through the development of new action plans.

There seems to be two general levels of action planning. At one level, there is planning that occurs within sessions (internal action planning) and, at another level, planning that occurs outside of counselling (external action planning). During a client's involvement in counselling, there can be considerable movement with respect to what is happening within particular counselling sessions–internal action planning. There also might be some limited use of external action planning. At the point of closure, however, there is usually some movement toward external action planning. It is this latter form of action planning which is generally acknowledged in the counselling literature.

Self Management

In everyday conversation, some people describe personal development using the metaphor of "learning to fish" as contrasted with being "given a fish"; the point is that people who learn techniques that they can use on their own are better equipped than those who do not. Learning these techniques, however, can take extra time and effort and there is always the temptation to proceed directly to solutions without learning the basic steps.

> *clients learn best through "doing" and taking responsibility for their own behaviour; to achieve this end ... you must be prepared to move from the role of direct service provider to one of a consultant to the learning process*

Many people would like to find their career direction with a minimum of effort. You may find that you are often placed on a pedestal and are asked to perform "miracles" to solve life/career problems. As you are well aware, however, there are no easy answers and clients must be prepared to put time and effort into finding their own solutions. Your role is to facilitate this exploration and to teach clients strategies for understanding themselves better and the labour market. According to Bezanson et al. (1985), to achieve this end, you must repeatedly use behaviours such as the following:

- Not doing for clients what they can do for themselves.

- Expecting clients to be responsible.

- Not asking for more than clients are capable of, but not settling for less either.

- Encouraging clients to take initiative.

5. Verbally rewarding and reinforcing positive efforts, resisting the temptation to "rescue" when clients flounder.

With this approach, there is the strong belief that clients learn best through "doing" and through taking responsibility for their own behaviour. To achieve this end, you must be prepared to move from the role of direct service provider to one in which you become a consultant to the learning process.

Within the role of consultant, you will need to utilize several broad strategies to enhance self management (Bezanson et al., 1985) The first strategy focuses on teaching clients how to monitor their own behaviour and how to ask for feedback from others. While the feedback you supply is very important, there also is a need to move beyond the comfortable counselling relationship to connections with others. Giving clients the opportunity to monitor and evaluate their own actions is an essential first step in this process. To supplement their self-monitoring efforts, they should be given instruction and encouraged to seek feedback from others (family members, friends, employers) regarding "how they are coming across to others."

As clients learn to monitor their own behaviours they will have to learn how not to become "bogged down" with negative self talk. We are often our own worst critics and this type of negative thinking serves only to undermine self confidence and reduce motivation. One aspect of self monitoring is to listen carefully to the messages we give ourselves about our ability to learn and to achieve results. People who struggle with success often can be heard using phrases such as the following:

"That's so stupid. I am never going to get it right."

"I can't believe I did that. When will I ever learn?"

People who are successful have learned to use more positive self talk and for them phrases such as the following are common:

"OK, so what went wrong here. I'll change my approach and see how this works."

"I've made this work before. I'll get it if I just keep trying."

Focusing self monitoring on self talk can help clients learn how to motivate themselves for success.

Another self-management strategy looks at problem solving and how to handle challenging situations. Rather than being overwhelmed by situations, clients can learn how to analyze what is happening and how to construct workable solutions. Within problem solving, there are important skills such as problem identification (narrowing the problem, isolating key elements), brainstorming, analyzing alternatives, visualization, and implementing actions. As was mentioned earlier, most clients come to counselling because they are "stuck." Helping them develop the skills to extricate themselves from difficult and unexpected situations is a good long-term coping strategy.

In our current global and information-based world, the need for ongoing learning throughout the life span is essential. You can encourage clients to continue the self-development process through involvement in a range of different learning possibilities. In making these long-term plans, you may find it important to focus on a logical progression of activities and also to choose activities which are challenging but not overwhelming to the client.

Perhaps the most important self-management strategy concerns the need for ongoing self care. We all need to find time for ourselves and also to attain a balance between our emotional, physical, cognitive, social, and spiritual needs. In our increasingly "busy" world, it is easy to lose sight of our priorities and find ourselves sliding downwards. Helping clients to look at their personal needs and also how to reward themselves can contribute to self-management. Bezanson et al. (1985) use questions such as the following to facilitate this exploration:

"What do you do for fun? What do you do to relax? What makes you feel good?"

"Of the things you do everyday, which would you hate to give up? Which would you like to keep?"

"What are your hobbies?"

"What people do you like to be with? What do you like to do with people?"

To explore personal needs (emotional, physical, cognitive, social and spiritual), you may find it helpful to use activities such as the pattern identification exercise (Chapter Four).

Self-management adds an extra dimension to the counselling process that contributes to long-term effectiveness. It also coincides with good counselling since much of the focus is on active client involvement, a central ingredient for client motivation and commitment. Effective application of self-management strategies depends on both the readiness of clients and the willingness of ourselves as counsellors to teach clients skills as well as provide them with answers.

Closing Ceremonies

The title "closing ceremonies" is perhaps too grand a notion for many counselling exchanges, but what I am hoping to capture here is the element of ceremony that helps to signify the closing of a chapter and the opening of new possibilities. In career counselling, we also need to include some ceremonial elements to honour what has been accomplished and to signify the coming changes through working out action planning.

Many traditional ending ceremonies include some sharing of food; and depending on the circumstances, this may be appropriate. It might only be a cupcake, but it does serve a significant function. Other ceremonies involve certificates of accomplishment; and, if this is appropriate to the situation, then some statement of completion could be put together. For some people it is more a reflection of what has been overcome. Problems can be placed on a piece of paper and then symbolically shredded or tossed into the waste basket. Some counsellors use candles and in the final moments take time to extinguish the light. At the risk of being overly dramatic, I do see all of these methods as having some utility depending on the nature of the relationship.

> *In career counselling, we need to include some ceremonial elements to honour what has been accomplished and to signify the coming changes through action planning.*

Summary

Of course, there will be any number of occasions where a simple handshake or hug might be all that is required. What is important is that the ending is recognized through some formal gesture. Endings deserve a special place within the counselling framework.

This chapter highlights the importance of endings within the counselling process. The metaphor of bookends can be used here to describe the way in which beginnings and endings help to contain and focus the shape of the counselling process. During this special time there is a review of client strengths and an acknowledgement of what has been accomplished. Feelings of loss and uncertainty also become part of this process and ceremonial actions help to mark the closure. Endings do not just mean a look backwards, however, and this is where connections are made to new beginnings. Action planning and self-management help to structure this new linkage and thus, become particularly important during the closing phase.

Chapter Eight makes the transition from counselling process to counsellor training. Helping counsellors to develop the necessary counselling competencies for the active engagement model presents some special challenges, and in this next chapter I have provided some suggestions based on my experiences as a counsellor educator.

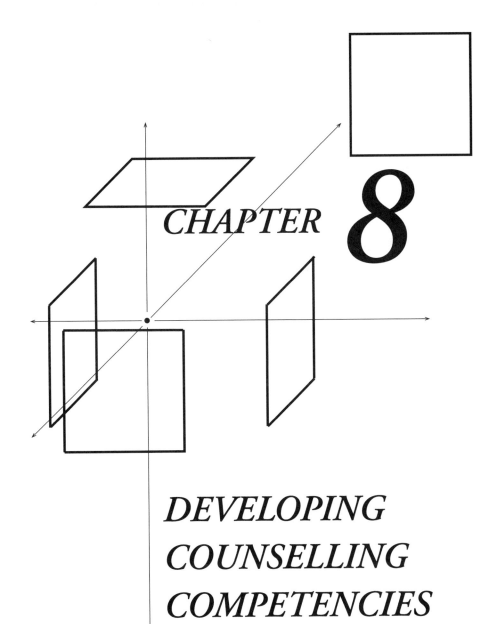

CHAPTER **8**

DEVELOPING COUNSELLING COMPETENCIES

The counselling model that has been presented in the preceding chapters reflects a somewhat different vision for career counselling, one in which imagination and creativity play a key role in counselling practice. Developing the counselling competencies for such an approach requires a broadly-based learning strategy. In this chapter, I will start by presenting a general model of competence and then move to more specific strategies that can be used to enhance learning.

A General Model of Competence

When considering the notion of competence with respect to counselling practice, I think that it is important to include a broad range of factors. Competence, as I see it, refers to a state of being as well as to a state of doing. While performance is a necessary by-product of competence, it is important to recognize that competence stretches far beyond immediate results. A competent person is one who has the capacity (or power) to deal adequately with emerging situations. In today's turbulent social and economic climate, this focus on the emerging situation is obviously of critical importance.

I have formulated a competence model (Figure Twelve) with eight components that has been the focus of some research by Professor Magda Ritook (1997), from Lorand Eotvos University in Hungary. This research is based on a competence-appraisal checklist (see Appendix Two), and her findings have supported the structure of such a model. Listed below are each of the major components of the model along with a brief description.

> *A competent person is one who has the capacity (or power) to deal adequately with emerging situations.*

1. Purpose

Motivation, commitment and initiative are triggered by a clear sense of direction and purpose. People are willing to devote themselves fully to tasks when they value what they are doing and see how they can make a positive contribution. You will need to develop a personal mission statement that reflects your general sense of purpose. With this foundation you will be able to meet personal and organizational challenges with integrity and confidence.

Figure Twelve: Competence Model

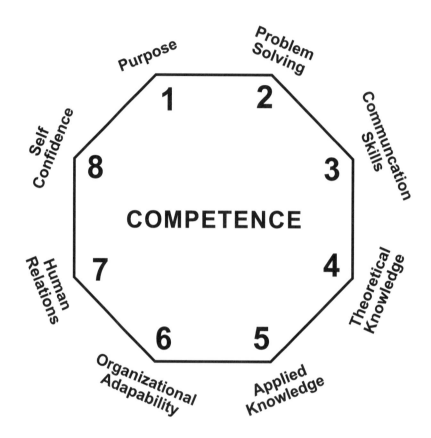

2. Problem Solving

The counselling model described in this book clearly highlights the need for good problem solving skills. These skills include the ability to abstract information from a wide variety of sources, to consider all aspects of an issue, to think creatively, to make sound judgments, and to construct effective action plans. People who are good problem solvers are able to think clearly under difficult circumstances. There is little doubt that the complexity of the issues that clients present has increased dramatically in recent years and problem solving is a much needed skill.

3. Communication Skills

The ability to communicate effectively with clients, colleagues, supervisors, and community members is a central building block in the development of counselling competence. Through communication skills, we express our ideas to one another (verbally, non-verbally and in written form) and incorporate the ideas of others into our perspective. Good communicators are able both to express understanding and to motivate others to action.

4. Theoretical Knowledge

The development and maintenance of up-to-date theoretical knowledge requires an involvement with learning that transcends the traditional academic preparation period. The necessity of learning throughout one's life span has become a reality, and you will need to be prepared to be involved in a variety of learning tasks (workshops, conferences, courses, general reading) to keep current. Acquiring knowledge also requires an efficient system of obtaining and organizing information so that it is readily accessible.

5. Applied Knowledge

As you attempt to integrate theory into practice, you will need to find access to practical situations where this can be accomplished. This practical experience must be structured in such a way that it contains elements of security, relevance, challenge, and critical reflection. In a secure environment, you need to feel free to take risks, make mistakes and, through this process, develop innovative ideas. Relevance is important because of its connection to the sense of purpose that was discussed earlier. Challenge will encourage you to set high standards and to stretch yourself to the limits of your abilities. Finally, critical reflection is important to maximize learning and to promote greater flexibility.

6. Organizational Adaptability

The organizational structures that surround us require a capacity to work within the system to achieve results. You will need to understand the written and unwritten rules by which organizations function and be able to use this knowledge (with integrity) to accomplish your goals. This capacity requires flexibility, an appreciation of change, and a willingness to work with colleagues and persons in authority. People with strength in this area are able to reframe problems and "make things happen."

7. Human Relations

Being able to build and nurture positive relationships is an obvious counselling attribute. Being an effective counsellor will require you to form relationships with people at many different levels. You will need to believe that people "matter," and through your actions, extend "mattering" to others (see Chapter Two). Part of building positive relationships is knowing how to ask for and receive feedback from others and how to give constructive feedback to others. The development of strong support networks encourages and promotes counselling effectiveness.

8. Self-Confidence

Self-confidence comes from past experiences, support, constructive feedback, successes, a sense of personal ability, and a willingness to move forward. To attain competence, you will need to feel confident to initiate action and take risks. You will need to find the inner strength to learn from mistakes and the motivation to persevere. This confidence often leads to leadership and mentoring opportunities.

The relationship between each of the components of the competence model is such that they all work together to create a unified whole. As was mentioned earlier, if you are interested in assessing your general competence levels you might find the competence appraisal checklist in Appendix Two a useful guide.

The competence model that has been presented has been applied specifically to the competence of counsellors. The model has wider application, however, and can also be applied to the competence levels of clients. In many respects, the goals of counselling are to promote many of the same factors that have been identified in the competence model. As you work with your clients, you may find it helpful to use the competence model to help them assess their relative strengths and weaknesses. This self-assessment may serve to highlight areas where there is a need for further growth and development.

Reflective Moments

The work of Schon (1983) and Anderson (1991) certainly points to the importance of using reflective moments within the counselling process. Creativity and good problem solving are closely tied to having the time to reflect upon what is happening and to formulate new responses. The spaces for this type of reflection are usually found only in the times between counselling sessions. Going back to the early section on conventions (Chapter Two), the point was made that perhaps there were other times within the counselling session where reflective moments could be inserted. This is not to say that reflection is not happening at all within the counselling session, rather that it is challenging for counsellors to focus completely on the client and at the same time be reflecting about possible hypotheses and new directions.

> *Creativity and good problem solving are closely tied to having the time to reflect upon what is happening and to formulate new responses.*

One of the ways in which reflection can be directly introduced into counselling sessions is to start by setting an expectation with respect to the sequence of activities within a typical counselling session. A statement from the counsellor such as the following fits this modality:

> *"What we are going to do today then is meet for about 40 minutes and then we will take a short break to assess what we have accomplished and where we will go from there."*

By normalizing this type of arrangement, you can help clients to expect the short break as part of the counselling process. At an appropriate point in the counselling session, you can then suggest that it is perhaps time for a brief period of reflection and indicate that you will be stepping outside the room for a few minutes. While you are "taking stock" of the situation and what to do next, you can encourage your client to think about what has been accomplished and future directions. Leaving the counselling room gives you time to consult with others (if appropriate) and also to think carefully about what has transpired. It is often helpful during these reflective moments to try to formulate a metaphor to capture the essential elements of what has occurred. The metaphor also can be helpful to suggest ways in which the counselling might proceed in a different direction. After the short break, no more than 5 minutes, you need to return to the room and share perspectives. Ask your client to share his/her perspective, and then you can share your ideas. Counsellors who have used this paraticular method have reported that the brief break allowed them to "clear their head" and helped them gain a better understanding of the counselling dynamics. The break seemed to be particularly helpful in situations where clients tended to "wander" and where counsellors felt the need for more structure.

> *Leaving the counselling room gives you time to consult with others (if appropriate) and also to think carefully about what has transpired.*

Anderson (1991) describes another approach using the idea of a reflective team. With this method, other counsellors observe (one-way mirrors) the counselling session and at an appropriate moment, the counselling is suspended and the observers change places with the counsellor and client. The observers then discuss their ideas about what has occurred and the counsellor and client step into the observational role and listen to the discussion. Following this, the client and counsellor come back into the counselling room and discuss their reactions to what they have heard. This exchange between client and counsellor and the observers can occur on several occasions during the course of counselling. While this approach can lead to some very interesting and exciting results, there are some cautions that must be heeded. There must be some initial discussion between counsellor and client beforehand to set the stage for this event. Persons in the observational role must also receive some instruction with respect to how to frame their comments when they step into the counselling room. This is a time for strength challenge and the discussion must be very carefully managed. The reflective team process is one that offers some exciting possibilities; but as with most powerful strategies, it must be applied with sensitivity and respect.

Outside of counselling sessions, counsellors can also benefit by finding time for some reflective moments. For some people, these moments are best utilized through quiet reflection; others benefit by being more active and writing down their thoughts on flip charts. Discussing the situation with others is also usually an effective method of sorting through the various facets of the counselling process.

The Three Faces of Empathy

Despite the emphasis in this book on counselling methods, one should not lose sight of the importance of empathy as one of the foundations of counselling practice. In most counselling programs, trainees are assumed to have the necessary empathy; the major learning task is to teach people how to express their empathy using statements such as "*You feel... because....*" While this is undoubtedly an important component of active listening training, at times it appears superficial and I wonder if we are only looking at outward manifestations. There certainly is no question that people differ dramatically in their ability to use empathy. What accounts for some of these differences?

Some of the work by Michael Schwalbe (1988) on role taking seems to have relevance for understanding the sources of empathy. According to Schwalbe (1988), there are three factors that account for some of the differences in empathy development.

The first factor, **ACCURACY**, refers to one's ability to understand the ideas and feelings of others accurately. Schwalbe postulates that accuracy comes from being in situations where people are powerless and are forced to focus on the wishes and feelings of others. Under these conditions, it is important to interpret accurately how others are perceiving a situation. When one looks at literature, there seems to be many stories of powerful rulers learning their "craft" by coming down from their positions of power and assuming the role of the ordinary folk. It seems that one can not learn how to deal with people solely from a position of power and influence. It is only by wearing the cloak of humility and powerlessness that true empathy is acquired. Applying this condition more

Learning to make empathic statements depends not only on active listening training but also on a variety of other experiences and reflections.

broadly, I think that it would be fair to say that the counsellor in many respects is placed in a special position of power. Being the "all knowing specialist" may run counter to empathy development. Counsellors seeking to enhance their empathy for others, at least with respect to accuracy, may need to seek out situations where they are relating to others without the trappings of their counselling role or reflect on times when they have been in need, perhaps times when they have faced challenges such as job loss.

A second empathy factor is that of **RANGE**. People may have good empathy skills but be restricted to a very narrow range. Expanding one's range of empathy depends on acquiring a variety of experiences with people from different backgrounds. Through contact with others different from ourselves, we learn to appreciate different perspectives on the world. Acquiring this knowledge is furthered through careful observation and by listening to the stories of others. Meeting people with diverse perspectives occurs through travel both within and outside of one's community. It is easy to get into a "rut" and only deal with a narrow band of people. As counsellors we have a unique opportunity to develop a special appreciation for the perspectives of others if we take the time to encourage and listen to the life stories of our clients.

The third and final empathy dimension is that of **DEPTH**. True empathy can cut beyond surface issues and focus on central life concerns. People learn depth through their involvement in meaningful relationships with others. Sensitivity is enhanced through experience and reflections on one's own interpersonal relationships. We need to have experienced mature relationship so that we can develop insights with respect to human behaviour.

Incorporating the concepts of accuracy, range and depth in counsellor training and development enriches the possibilities for empathy training. Life experience and reflection become key ingredients which form the very basis of empathy. Learning to make empathic statements depends not only on active listening training but also on a variety of other experiences and reflections. As one illustration of this search for empathic understanding, you might reflect upon a condensed version of a poem entitled "Embracing the Mystery" written by Sumiko Nishizawa:

> I left for Canada to search for unknowns
> to better understand the children
>   in my elementary classroom.
> There had become awkward space between them and me

I used to feel I understood them well
Forty Japanese children filled with energy
Every morning, they would come to me and tell me their stories
Fascinating stories about green turtles, a crescent moon,
   or baked potatoes on a plate.

After years and years, I thought
     I knew how to listen to them
     I knew how to talk with them
     I knew how to teach
In my small world,
I thought I understood my children

One day a girl joined my class.
She looked just like the others
But she had been to school in New York for three years.
She was lively, unique and chatty,
different from the others.
I tried to re-form her, to fit her to my class
She became quiet.

One day I met a Korean-Japanese girl
she was shy, silent
her parents were concerned that she be safe

I did not understand
why they worried so much
she smiled towards the end of the year
but remained silent

Cultures, language, ethnicity,
what did I know about the world?

> I quit teaching and left for Canada to search for unknowns
> to better understand the children
>   in my elementary classroom
> There had become awkward space between them and me

After five years of living in Canada
I begin to feel
the energetic spirit of the girl from the U.S.
the fear of racism of the Korean-Japanese girl
I know now what it is like to be apart from the majority

I am still searching for unknowns and uncertainties
still striving to embrace all students in my classroom
I am still learning about the world
still hoping to teach them the width and depth of the world.

In this poem, Ms. Nishizawa shares with us her struggle to understand others and her commitment to broadening her perspective. Through her experiences, she is determined to expand her awareness of the world and to grasp the life realities of those around her. While we are not all called to such dramatic career shifts, the need to confront our own "small worlds" is compelling.

Putting the Counselling Model into Practice

It is one thing to read about various counselling strategies and attitudes and something else to begin putting them into practice. As a counselling supervisor, I have observed a number of problems as students have tried to incorporate this counselling approach into their counselling practice. One problem that was mentioned earlier is the difficulty that some people have in moving beyond problem definition. When this occurs there is good use of active listening skills, including empathy, but an inability to set a clear counselling direction. Rather than moving forward, the counselling process seems to turn in on itself and the discussion goes in circles. Breaking free from this problem is often related to building self confidence and encouraging risk taking. Counsellors in training need to operate from a sense of safety and need to be encouraged to express and act upon their intuitive hunches (Amundson, Poehnell & Smithson, 1996). Beliefs about a lack of creativity and imagination also need to be challenged. Research on creativity would suggest that people frequently under utilize their creative potential because of negative prior learning and fear about openly expressing themselves (Epstein, 1996; Sternberg & Lubart, 1995).

> *Counsellors in training need to operate from a sense of safety and need to be encouraged to express and act upon their intuitive hunches*

A very different type of problem occurs when people become too enthusiastic about the various problem-resolving tasks and lose sight of the counselling relationship and the nature of the problem. Often counsellors facing this challenge are keen to incorporate new strategies but are unwilling to invest the time and energy to have a solid foundation from which to explore. Under these conditions, clients may feel confused and unsure about the agenda of the counsellor. To minimize problems in this domain, counsellors need to reduce their reliance on strategies and relax with the counselling process. Rather than hurrying through the problem definition phase, they should allow themselves sufficient time to explore all aspects of the client's story.

Connected to the problem just mentioned is the situation where counsellors want to fill their sessions with various problem-resolving tasks. In this scenario, the utilization of strategies becomes an end in itself and there is a tendency to "skip along the surface" without any real depth. Rather than realizing the full power of a particular strategy, counsellors find themselves moving too quickly to something else. Counselling strategies are not designed to be an end in themselves; effective counsellors recognize this fact and have the wisdom and patience to employ strategies accordingly.

A final problem that I have observed occurs when counsellors are helping clients to make the transition from problem definition to problem resolution. Many counsellors find that when they go to make the transition, they set their empathy skills aside and focus more on the parameters of the particular strategy. This is particularly the case when counsellors are first learning new resolution strategies and find themselves concentrating more on what is going to happen than what is happening before them. Empathy is not something that can be turned off at any point in the counselling process. As I mentioned earlier, empathy is the foundation of counselling and needs to be ever present.

With practice, counsellors learn to maintain a high level of empathy with clients while at the same time they are introducing more active strategies. It is this integration which is the heart of the active engagement counselling model.

Audio/Video Playback

There is little doubt that audio/video playback helps counsellors improve their counselling skills. Schon (1983) discusses the importance of becoming a reflective practitioner and technology can help us with that process. As counsellors see and hear themselves in action, they can begin to evaluate their counselling effectiveness. In evaluating counselling tapes, I encourage counsellors to look at the positive as well as the negative. Many counsellors can become fixated on what didn't go well and never tune in to the moments when they are effective.

> *As counsellors see and hear themselves in action, they can begin to evaluate their counselling effectiveness.*

When looking for positive illustrations of client behaviours, counsellors are well advised to listen carefully (to both verbal and non-verbal cues) for instances of what I have called "moments of movement." The following quotes are some illustrations of client statements which illustrate moments of movement:

"When I first came here, I had no idea that counselling would be so involved. Seeing that Wheel really puts everything into a different perspective."

"I always saw myself as someone who couldn't relate to people. The exercise today has really got me thinking about this. Maybe I have been looking at this in the wrong way. Just because I don't like being the leader of a group doesn't mean that I don't like people."

*"I never realized that there were so many careers in the
medical field. I used to think just about being a doctor or
nurse, but it's a lot bigger than that."*

*"Seeing myself on videotape during the interviewing exercise
was a real eye opener. I couldn't believe how often I looked at
my notes whenever I was asked a question."*

*"Seeing it put together in this way is really interesting.
Everything does seem to be pointing towards either social
work or nursing. I guess it's time to make a decision."*

You will note from the examples that moments of movement can be
very small changes in perspective. Not everything is an *"Ah Ha"*
experience and we need to pay attention to the small movements as well
as to the major shifts. Learning to facilitate and monitor "moments of
movement" is an important skill in counselling. Often counsellors are
aware at some level that change is occurring, but are unable to articulate
clearly the specific moments of client movement. Practising this skill
helps to develop a greater awareness of the counselling process and how
change is happening.

The availability and practical utility of audio/video playback is
something which just doesn't fit well into some settings. In situations
where taping is not possible, I suggest that counsellors approach the
review process in a slightly different manner. Using a process called
interpersonal-process recall, counsellors should mentally review what
occurred in the selected session immediately afterwards and then take
some time to make detailed notes of their observations (or use a tape
recorder to record their descriptions). Rather than introducing any
specific form of interpretation, I have simply asked counsellors to
describe what occurred during the counselling session and then to reflect
upon the counselling process using the notes as the stimulus for critical
self evaluation.

Direct Supervisory Input

In most formal counselling training, there are some options for supervision using observation through a one way glass or audio/video playback. Counsellors in the field, however, often do not have access to these forms of feedback. Under these conditions, the main form of feedback from others usually comes through discussions of case dynamics. I found myself working in a situation where there was not easy access to one way mirrors or recording equipment and in this setting developed a direct supervisory approach which seemed to work well. What I discovered was that there were some things that you could do using this approach that went beyond the usual supervisory efforts. Prior to discussing some of the advantages and limitations, however, I would like to briefly describe my three-step supervisory procedure.

1. Setting the Stage

The counsellor would inform his/her client about the counselling process, which includes regular visits from a supervisor (I have found that most clients have no problems with this structure as long as the counsellor is not overly anxious about the visits). The key point here is the fact that the visits are part of a regular routine and, therefore, not a reflection of anything special happening. The counsellor also assures the client that if in any way the timing for the supervisory visit is not appropriate then this will be respected. A brief introductory visit with the supervisor is also included to help establish the relationship.

2. The Counselling Visit

At a point in the middle of the second session, the supervisor knocks on the door and asks if this is a good time for a visit. As I mentioned above, the supervisor only enters the room at the invitation of the counsellor and client. If the timing is good, the counsellor will summarize what has occurred (checking with the client) and then continue with the counselling process. The supervisor usually assumes an observational role and only responds when invited. At the end of the observation sequence (about 15 minutes), the supervisor comments how everything seems to be going well and leaves the counselling session. Further visits may occur on a similar basis during subsequent counselling sessions.

There may be some occasions when there is a need for the supervisor to move beyond observation to direct intervention. Again, respecting the relationship between counsellor and client, the supervisor may in these instances engage the client by providing information or by using a particular counselling strategy. These moments of direct intervention should be well timed and serve as meaningful demonstrations. It is very important during the counselling sessions for the supervisor not to take control away from the counsellor.

3. Debriefing

As with any other form of supervision, ongoing discussions are advisable. In these meetings it is important for the supervisor not only to focus on what he or she personally observed but also to consider the case in its entirety. With this in mind, counsellor and supervisor should be aware of how the observed segments may be similar or different from other counselling dynamics.

In using this direct supervisory approach, I have become aware of both advantages and some limitations. On the plus side, there certainly is something to be gained through direct observation and modelling. There is something special about being "in the room" that is lost through any other means of observation, i.e. one way mirrors, audio or videotaping. Some of the limitations focus on the disruption that occurs whenever a new person enters the room. With practice and sensitivity, I have learned to minimize this element, but it still can be an important factor. Also, the issue of not undermining the counsellor's authority in the counselling relationship is something that must always be monitored.

Metaphoric Case Conceptualization

Throughout this book, the use of metaphors has been highlighted as a means of both expressing and resolving client problems. Metaphors are visual containers into which a complex array of information can be placed. Through understanding and changing metaphors, you can help clients develop new insights.

I have extended the use of metaphors to case conceptualization because of the synthesis that is possible through the use of visual images (Amundson, 1988). Some research by Stone and Amundson (1989) has also supported the use of this particular method in counsellor training.

The first step in this method is to have counsellors describe their clients in metaphoric images, i.e. someone lost in a fog, a person trying to juggle too many balls.

One of the advantages of having metaphors expressed through drawings is that there is something very concrete on which to focus.

These images can be simply discussed or expressed through drawings. Once the images are clearly in mind, I ask the counsellors to consider how they might fit themselves into the situation. Using one example, a counsellor indicated that he viewed his client as having too many "balls in the air." When he thought of himself within the image, he felt that he was in a position where he was picking up the balls that had fallen to the floor.

Once the image is clearly defined, counsellors can begin to analyze the different elements of the image that have been created. The five key factors to be explored are as follows:

"(a) the sense of **direction** with respect to the counselling process;

(b) the level of **optimism** that the counsellor has when considering possible outcomes;

(c) the closeness and nature of the client-counsellor **relationship**;

(d) the extent to which the counsellor feels **responsible** for the problem; and

(e) the level of **potency** which the counsellor feels when assessing counselling interventions."
(Amundson, 1988, p.392)

Continuing with the example of the counsellor picking up balls that the client had dropped to the floor, you can see that the counsellor has a sense of direction but perhaps it might not be the most desired one. There certainly is a sense of futility (lack of potency) and pessimism reflected in the image. The counsellor and client are working together, but the nature of the relationship is not really that close. The counsellor seems to be assuming most of the responsibility for solving the problems (the dropped balls) that are occurring.

Changing the metaphor can alter some of the dynamics inherent in the situation. Suppose for instance that the counsellor stopped picking up the balls and let the situation take its course for awhile. Problems might intensify in the short term, but the client might come away with a more realistic sense of capacity. As a follow-up to this situation, the counsellor might do well to help the client focus on the more important balls and/or develop better strategies for juggling.

One of the advantages of having metaphors expressed through drawings is that there is something very concrete on which to focus.

Many counsellors share their drawings with their clients as well as use the drawings as a basis for the case conceptualization activity. In this respect the drawing becomes another counselling tool to help clients better understand their situation (in this case, how they are being perceived by the counsellor). It also can be interesting to compare the metaphors that clients have for themselves and how they are being perceived by others. Of course, the major point of the metaphoric case conceptualizaton exercise is to help counsellors better understand the dynamics of the counselling relationship.

Summary

Learning to be an effective counsellor is an ongoing process. The various elements contained in the competence model illustrate the broadly-based nature of this development. In many respects, one never "arrives" and the pleasure comes as much from the journey as the place.

I have continually pointed to the importance of creativity and imagination and see these personal attributes as essential elements in the counselling process. As Roger's core conditions of respect, empathy and genuineness are experienced within the expanse of creativity and imagination, one can begin to connect with the "art" as well as the science of counselling. Career counselling must be conceived within a broader and more flexible base if it is to have relevance to clients struggling with the uncertainty of our current situation.

The flexibility that I am addressing here extends to many different levels. At the most basic level there is the question of how career counselling differs from personal counselling. Authors such as Herr (1997) are pointing the way toward a greater fusion between career and personal counselling. With respect to counselling practice, the active engagement model certainly suggests the need to examine existing counselling conventions and to incorporate a more active and imaginative counselling approach.

The focus in this last chapter has been on the personal and professional development of the counsellor. Counsellor education and development must go hand in hand with new counselling methods. It is in this area that I have found the most challenge. It is too easy to follow a well-trodden path, even when it is going in the wrong direction. Hopefully the writing of this book will focus attention on the need for a new vision to enhance some aspects of the career counselling process.

References

Amundson, N. E. (1979). Using projective techniques in career counselling. *Canadian Counsellor, 13,* 225-229.

Amundson, N. E. (1984). Career counselling with primary group involvement. *Canadian Counsellor, 18,* 180-183.

Amundson, N. E. (1988). The use of metaphor and drawings in case conceptualization. *Journal of Counseling and Development, 66,* 391-393.

Amundson, N. E. (1989a). A model of individual career counseling. *Journal of Employment Counseling, 26,* 132-138.

Amundson, N. E. (1989b). *Individual style survey.* Edmonton, Alberta: Psychometrics Canada.

Amundson, N. E. (1994). Negotiating identity during unemployment. *Journal of Employment Counseling, 31,* 98-104.

Amundson, N. E. (1995a). An interactive model of career decision making. *Journal of Employment Counseling, 32,* 11-21.

Amundson, N. E. (1995b). Pattern identification exercise. *ERIC Digest,* EDD-CG-95-69, Greensboro, NC: ERIC/CASS.

Amundson, N. E., & Borgen, W. A. (1987). Coping with unemployment: What helps and hinders. *Journal of Employment Counseling, 24,* 97-106.

Amundson, N. E., & Kenney, S. (1979). The non-voluntary client. Unpublished Manuscript, Vancouver: The University of British Columbia.

Amundson, N. E., & Penner, K. (in press). Parent involved career exploration. *The Career Development Quarterly.*

Amundson, N. E., & Poehnell, G. (1996). *Career pathways* (2nd ed.). Richmond, B.C.: Ergon Communications

Amundson, N. E., & Poehnell, G. (1998). *Career pathways: Quick trip.* Richmond, BC: Ergon Communications.

Amundson, N. E., Poehnell, G., & Smithson, S. (1996). *Employment counselling theory and strategies: A book of readings.* Richmond, BC: Ergon Communications.

Amundson, N. E., Westwood, M., & Prefontaine, R. (1995). Cultural bridging and employment counselling with clients from different cultural backgrounds. *Canadian Journal of Counselling, 29,* 206-213.

Anderson, T. (1991). *The reflecting team: Dialogues and dialogues about the dialogues.* New York: Norton.

Azrin, N. H., Flores, T., & Kaplan, S. J. (1975). Job-finding club: A group assisted program for obtaining employment. *Behavior Research and Therapy, 13,* 17-27.

Berne, E. (1964). *Games people play.* New York: Ballantine Books.

Bezanson, M. L., DeCoff, C. A., & Stewart, N. R. (1985). *Individual employment counselling: An action based approach.* Toronto: Guidance Centre.

Bird, B. J. (1989). *Entrepreneurial behaviour.* London, UK: Scott, Foresman & Company.

Borgen, A. W., Pollard, D. E., Amundson, N. E., & Westwood, M. J. (1989). *Employment groups: The counseling connection.* Toronto: Lugus.

Borgen, W. A., & Amundson, N. E. (1987). The dynamics of unemployment. *Journal of Counseling and Development, 66,* 180-184.

Borgen, W. A., & Amundson, N. E. (1996). *Starting points with youth.* Victoria, BC: MEOST.

Borgen, W. A., & Amundson, N. E. (1996). Strength challenge as a process for supervision. *Counselor Education and Supervision, 36,* 159-169.

Boy, A. V., & Pine, G. J. (1990). *A person-centered foundation for counseling and psychotherapy.* Springfield, IL: Charles C. Thomas.

Brower, D., & Weider, L. (1950). Projective techniques in business and industry. In L. E. Abt & L. Bellak (Eds.), *Projective psychology.* New York: Grove Press.

Burton, M. L., & Wedemeyer, R. A. (1991). *In transition.* New York: Harper Business.

Combs, G., & Freedman, J. (1990). *Symbol, story & ceremony.* New York: Norton.

de Shazer, S. (1985). *Keys to solution in brief therapy.* New York: Norton.

de Bono, E. (1985). *Six thinking hats.* Boston: Little, Brown.

Egan, G. (1986). *The skilled helper: Models, skills, and methods for effective helping* (3rd Ed.). Pacific Grove, CA: Brooks/Cole.

Foster, R. J. (1978). *Celebration of discipline: The path to spiritual growth.* New York: Harper & Row.

Friedman, S. (Ed.). (1993). *The new language of change*. New York: The Guilford Press.

Fritz, R. (1991). *Creating*. New York: Fawcett Columbine.

Gati, I. (1986). Making career decisions: A sequential elimination approach. *Journal of Counseling Psychology, 33*, 408-417.

Gelatt, H. B. (1989). Positive uncertainty: A new decision-making framework for counseling. *Journal of Counseling Psychology, 33*, 252-256.

Gelatt, H. B. (1991). *Creative decision making*. Los Altos, CA: Crisp Publications.

Gelso, C. J., & Carter, J. A. (1985). The relationship in counseling and psychotherapy: Components, consequences, and theoretical antecedents. *The Counseling Psychologist, 13*(2), 155-244.

Gilbert, D. T., & Cooper, J. (1985). Social psychological strategies of self-deception. In M. W. Martin (Ed.), *Self deception and self understanding* (pp. 75-94). Lawrence: University Press of Kansas.

Goldman, L. (1992). Qualitative assessment: An approach for counselors. *Journal of Counseling and Development, 70*, 616-621.

Gysbers, N. C., & Moore, E. J. (1987). *Career counseling skills and techniques for practitioners*. Boston: Allyn & Bacon.

Hammer, E. F. (1958). *The clinical application of projective drawing*. Springfield, IL: Charles C. Thomas.

Handy, C. (1994). *The age of paradox*. Boston: Harvard Business School Press.

Herr, E. L. (1993). Contexts and influences on the need for personal flexibility for the 21st century (part I). *Canadian Journal of Counselling, 27*, 148-164.

Herr, E. L. (1997). Perspectives on career guidance and counseling in the 21st century. *Educational and Vocational Guidance Bulletin, 60*, 1-15.

Holland, J. L. (1985a). *Making vocational choices: A theory of vocational personalities and work environments* (2nd ed.). Englewood Cliffs, NJ: Prentice-Hall.

Holland, J. (1985b). *The self-directed search: Professional manual*. Odessa, FL: Psychological Assessment Resources.

Kershaw, C. F. (1980). An introduction to graphology. Unpublished paper. Vancouver, B.C.

Lakoff, G., & Johnson, M. (1980). *Metaphors we live by.* Chicago: The University of Chicago Press.

Levy, S. (1950). Figure drawing as a projective test. In L. E. Abt & L. Bellak (Eds.), *Projective psychology.* New York: Grove Press.

Lindzey, G. (1952). The thematic apperception test: Interpretive assumptions and related empirical evidence. *Psychological Bulletin, 49,* 1-25.

McCormick, R. M., & Amundson, N. E. (1997). A career-life planning model for First Nations people. *Journal of Employment Counseling, 34,* 171-179.

Moses, B. (1997). *Career intelligence.* Toronto: Stoddart.

Mossop, C. (1994). *Values cards.* Toronto: Mossop, Cornelissen Consultants, Inc.

Murphy, G. (1947). *Personality.* New York: Harper & Row.

Myers, I. B., & McCaulley, M. H. (1985). *Manual: A guide to the development and use of the Myers-Briggs Indicator.* Palo Alto, CA: Consulting Psychologists Press.

O'Hanlon, W. H., & Weiner-Davis, M. (1989). *In search of solutions: A new direction in psychotherapy.* New York: Norton.

Patsula, P. (1992). *The assessment component of employment counselling.* Ottawa: Human Resources Development Canada.

Pedersen, P. (1993). *Culture-centered counseling skills.* New York: Homework.

Pedersen, P. (1997). *Culture-centered counselling interventions.* London: Sage.

Plant, P. (1997). Careerist, wage-earner, or entrepreneur: Work values and counseling. *Journal of Employment Counseling, 34,* 165-170.

Redekopp, D. E., Day, B., Magnusson, K., & Durnford, C. (1993). *Creating self-portraits.* Edmonton, AB: Centre for Career Development Innovation.

Reid, A. (1996). *Shakedown: How the new economy is changing our lives.* Toronto: Doubleday.

Rico, G. L. (1983). *Writing the natural way.* New York: J. P. Tarcher.

Rogers, C. R. (1951). *Client-centered therapy*. Boston: Houghton-Mifflin.

Rogers, C. R. (1961). *On becoming a person*. Boston: Houghton-Mifflin.

Rogers, C. R. (1980). *A way of being*. Boston: Houghton-Mifflin.

Sampson, J. P., Kolodinsky, R. W., & Greeno, B. P. (1997). Counseling on the information highway: Future possibiliites and potential problems. *Journal of Counseling and Development, 75*, 203-212.

Savickas, M. L. (1997). The spirit in career counseling. In D. P. Block, & L. J. Richmond (Eds.), *Connections between spirit of work in career development* (pp. 3-25). Palo Alto, CA: Davies-Black.

Schein, E. H. (1992). Career anchors and job/role planning: The links between career planning and career development. In D. H. Montross & C. J. Shinkman (Eds.), *Career development: Theory and practice*. Springfield, IL: C.C. Thomas.

Schlossberg, N. K., & Robinson, S. P. (1996). *Going to plan B*. New York: Simon & Schuster.

Schlossberg, N. K., Lassalle, A., & Golec. R. (1988). *The mattering scale for adults in higher education* (6th ed.). College Park, MD: University of Maryland.

Schlossberg, N. K., Lynch, A. Q., & Chickering, A. W (1989). *Improving higher education environments for adults*. San Francisco, CA: Jossey-Bass.

Schon, D. A. (1983). *The reflective practitioner*. New York: Basic Books.

Stone, D., & Amundson, N. (1989). Counsellor supervision: An exploratory study of the metaphoric case drawing method of case presentation in a clinical setting. *Canadian Journal of Counselling, 23*, 360-371.

Super, D. E., Osborne, W. L., Walsh, D. J., Brown, S. D., & Niles, S. G. (1992). Developmental career assessment and counseling: The C-DAC model. *Journal of Counseling and Development, 71*, 74-82.

Talmon, M. (1990). *Single-session therapy*. San Francisco: Jossey-Bass.

U.S. Employment Service (1979). *The General Aptitude Test Battery (GATB)*. Washington, DC: Author.

Vahamottonen, T. (1998). Reframing career counselling in terms of counsellor-client negotiations. Doctoral dissertation, University of Joensuu, Finland.

Vahamottonen, T., Keskinen, P. A., & Parrila, R. K. (1994). A conceptual framework for developing an activity-based approach to career counselling. *International Journal for the Advancement of Counselling, 17,* 19-34.

Walter, J. L., & Peller, J. E. (1992). *Becoming solution-focused in brief therapy.* New York: Brunner/Mazel.

Weinrach, S. G., & Thomas, K. R. (1996). The counseling profession's commitment to diversity-sensitive counseling: A critical reassessment. *Journal of Counseling and Development, 73,* 472-477.

Westwood, M. J. (1994). Developing skills for social-cultural competencies. Unpublished manuscript. UBC, Vancouver.

Westwood, M. J., & Ishiyama, F. I. (1991). Challenges in counseling immigrant clients: Understanding intercultural barriers to career adjustment. *Journal of Employment Counseling, 28,* 130-143.

Westwood, M., Amundson, N. E., & Borgen, W. A., Bailey, B., & Davies, G. (1994). *Starting points: Finding your route to employment.* Ottawa: Human Resources Development Canada.

White, M., & Epston, D. (1990). *Narrative means to therapeutic ends.* New York: Norton.

Wurman, R. S. (1989). *Information anxiety.* New York: Doubleday.

Young, R. E., Becker, A. L., & Pike, K. L. (1970). *Rhetoric: Discovery and change.* New York: Harcourt Brace Jovanovich.

Appendix One:

Ways of Mattering Questionnaire, Scoring Guide and Interpretation Guide

WAYS OF MATTERING QUESTIONNAIRE

Norman E. Amundson, Ph.D.

The University of British Columbia

© 1993

This questionnaire focuses on some of the ways you perceive your relationships with others. You will be asked to think about a specific person and then respond to a series of questions that describe aspects of that relationship. Of particular interest is the extent to which you feel that you are important or matter within this relationship. Think carefully about **each question** and choose the number that **BEST** describes **how often** each one **occurs** in your **RELATIONSHIP** using the following **FIVE POINT SCALE: 1 = Very Seldom; 2 = Seldom; 3= Sometimes; 4 = Often; 5 = Very Often.**

Situation: Indicate below the **person** that you are **referring** to when making this assessment:

Circle the number that BEST describes how often the person responds in the following ways:

1 = Very Seldom;   2 = Seldom;   3 = Sometimes;
4 = Often;   5 = Very Often

Examples: He/She ...

(a)   takes my feelings into account.   1   2   3   4   5

If you think this **describes your experience**, and the person usually **DOES take your FEELINGS into account**, then you would circle a '4' or '5'. IF, on the other hand, you think that **he/she DOESN'T take your FEELINGS into account** you would circle a '1' or '2'.

(b)   treats me like a number.   1   2   3   4   5

If you feel this **describes your experience**, and the person usually **TREATS you like a NUMBER**, then you would circle a '4' or '5'. On the other hand, **IF this is NOT the case** then you would **mark** a '1' or '2'.

He/She ...	Very Seldom	Seldom	Sometimes	Often	Very Often
(A) takes my feelings into account	1	2	3	4	5
(B) treats me like a number	1	2	3	4	5
(C) greets me in a way that makes me feel insignificant	1	2	3	4	5
(D) depends on me to give ideas	1	2	3	4	5
(E) has little interest in following my progress	1	2	3	4	5
(F) is indifferent to my contributions	1	2	3	4	5
(G) supports me in reaching my goals	1	2	3	4	5
(H) doesn't listen to what I have to say	1	2	3	4	5
(I) helps me to feel at ease	1	2	3	4	5
(J) doesn't depend on my participation	1	2	3	4	5
(K) takes into account what I want to do	1	2	3	4	5
(L) notices how I am feeling	1	2	3	4	5

(M) relies on my support	1	2	3	4	5
(N) cares little about my well being	1	2	3	4	5
(O) isn't interested in hearing about my future plans	1	2	3	4	5
(P) believes in me	1	2	3	4	5
(Q) will continue to be interested in me even when we go our separate ways	1	2	3	4	5
(R) doesn't make an effort to make me feel welcome	1	2	3	4	5
(S) doesn't appreciate what I have accomplished	1	2	3	4	5
(T) follows up to see how I am doing	1	2	3	4	5
(U) acknowledges my presence when entering the room	1	2	3	4	5
(V) has accepted few of my suggestions	1	2	3	4	5
(W) is careful to get my input before making decisions that affect me	1	2	3	4	5
(X) has little personal interest in keeping track of me	1	2	3	4	5

WAYS OF MATTERING
SCORING GUIDE

Norman E. Amundson, Ph.D.

The University of British Columbia

© 1993

Scoring

The ways of mattering questionnaire can be divided into four sub-scales with six items in each. The sub-scales are as follows:

Attention - The feeling that another person notices or is interested in you.

Importance - Others seem to care about what you want, think and do.

Dependence - You feel that you are a contributing member and others are counting on your participation.

Ego-extension - You believe that others are interested in your successes and disappointments and actively follow your progress.

The items in the questionnaire are written in such a way that half of them are phrased in a positive direction (e.g., taken my feelings into account), and half in a negative direction (e.g., treats me like a number). To obtain an overall positive score it is necessary to reverse the scoring of the items that are written in the negative direction. The reversal would go as follows: 5 becomes 1; 4 becomes 2; 3 stays as 3; 2 becomes 4; and 1 becomes 5. Score each of the following sub-scales, making the reversals where necessary.

Example:

Attention Sub-Scale

Item	Score		Positive Score
(i)	5	same	5
(l)	4	same	4
(u)	3	same	3
(b)	4	reversal	2
(c)	3	reversal	3
(r)	1	reversal	<u>5</u>

Total: <u>2</u>

Scoring Guide:

Attention Sub-Scale

Item	Score		Positive Score
(i)	_____	same	_____
(l)	_____	same	_____
(u)	_____	same	_____
(b)	_____	reversal	_____
(c)	_____	reversal	_____
(r)	_____	reversal	_____
		Total:	_____

Importance Sub-Scale

Item	Score		Positive Score
(a)	_____	same	_____
(g)	_____	same	_____
(k)	_____	same	_____
(h)	_____	reversal	_____
(n)	_____	reversal	_____
(s)	_____	reversal	_____
		Total:	_____

Dependence Sub-Scale

Item	Score	Positive Score	
(d)	_____	same	_____
(m)	_____	same	_____
(w)	_____	same	_____
(f)	_____	reversal	_____
(j)	_____	reversal	_____
(v)	_____	reversal	_____
		Total:	_____

Ego-Extension Sub-Scale

Item	Score	Positive Score	
(p)	_____	same	_____
(q)	_____	same	_____
(t)	_____	same	_____
(e)	_____	reversal	_____
(o)	_____	reversal	_____
(x)	_____	reversal	_____
		Total:	_____

Overall Positive Score

Attention   _____
Importance   _____
Dependence   _____
Ego-Extension   _____

Total: _____

WAYS OF MATTERING
INTERPRETATION GUIDE

Norman E. Amundson, Ph.D.

The University of British Columbia

© 1993

Understanding the information contained within the "Ways of Mattering" Questionnaire requires a careful review of the various sub-scales (Attention, Importance, Dependence, Ego-Extension) and the specific items which contribute to each area. The key information may be reflected by the total score, but in many cases a more in-depth review is necessary. Listed below are each of the sub-scales with the accompanying items:

ATTENTION: The feeling that another person notices or is interested in you.

Positive

I.   *helps me to feel at ease*
l.   *notices how I am feeling*
u.   *acknowledges my presence when entering the room*

Negative
b.   *treats me like a number*
c.   *greets me in ways that make me feel insignificant*
r.   *doesn't make an effort to make me feel welcome*

IMPORTANCE: Others seem to care about what you want, think, and do.

Positive

a. *takes my feelings into account*
g. *supports me in reaching my goals*
k. *takes into account what I want to do*

Negative

h. *doesn't listen to what I have to say*
n. *cares little about my well being*
s. *doesn't appreciate what I have accomplished*

DEPENDENCE: You feel that you are a contributing member and others are counting on your participation.

Positive

d. *depends on me to give ideas*
m. *relies on my support*
w. *is careful to get my input before making decisions that affect me*

Negative

f. *is indifferent to my contributions*
j. *doesn't depend on my participation*
v. *has accepted few of my suggestions*

EGO-EXTENSION: You believe that others are interested in your successes and disappointments and actively follow your progress.

Positive

p. *believes in me*
q. *will continue to be interested in me even when we go our separate ways*
t. *follows up to see how I am doing*

Negative

e. *has little interest in following my progress*
o. *isn't interested in hearing about my future plans*
x. *has little personal interest in keeping track of me*

When reviewing each of these items and sub-scales think about the particular situation(s) that contribute to either a high or low score. What are the specific circumstances that influence your feelings of mattering?

Depending on the circumstances surrounding the taking of the test, you may also have the opportunity to compare your results with others. If you do make this comparison, keep in mind that there are no right or wrong opinions with respect to feelings of mattering. What is of interest, are the differences and similarities between your perceptions and those of others.

Perhaps the key point to keep in mind when reflecting upon this questionnaire is the fact that your own personal self worth and sense of mattering do not depend on the mattering perspectives of other people. **You are an important and significant person whether or not you are treated as such by those around you.** However, it is not always easy to keep this perspective if you find yourself in situations where you are not receiving positive mattering messages. Being in a non-mattering situation usually requires extra energy, and it can slowly "eat away" at your self esteem and confidence. Because of the potential long term negative effects of non-mattering, it is essential to either change the nature of mattering relationships or leave the situation and seek out a more positive mattering climate.

Turning first to "changing mattering relationship," keep in mind that mattering is a "two-way street." Thus, it may be possible to increase mattering actions from others by changing your own behaviour. To what extent are you working hard, expressing yourself, and taking the initiative that will make others take note of your presence? Many people lie quietly like pearls within an oyster shell waiting to be discovered. This inaction is justified by the belief that to be visible would require action which would be a form of "brown-nosing" and would serve to reduce personal dignity. This perception needs to be challenged and looked at from a different point of view. Becoming visible to others is a necessity in today's fast paced society. Learning to "market" yourself in ways that reflect honesty and integrity may be the keys to higher levels of mattering. Also using your initiative and networking skills to contact and share information with friends, colleagues and those in authority may be essential in raising your profile.

Another way of approaching this situation is to look at how you are extending mattering to others. Are you following the golden rule and "treating others as you would like to be treated." Your generosity in being empathic and valuing the input of others helps to increase your own sensitivity and often has a way of being reflected back to yourself. It is through the act of unconditional giving and helping others that you may find a foundation for your own personal sense of mattering.

As was mentioned above, it is not always possible to alter the quality of mattering within a relationship. If you have **truly** extended yourself and still find that the relationship does not change, you may need to consider finding other relationships where you will receive the mattering that you need. Minimal contact or separation under these circumstances should not be viewed as failure since mattering depends on involvement and interaction of two parties. In moving away, however, it is important to not burn bridges and to remain open to renewing the relationship if the situation should change.

Appendix Two:

Competence Appraisal Checklist

Competence Appraisal Checklist

Assessing personal self-competence can be very challenging. The Competence Appraisal Checklist is designed to assist you with this task. When considering the following items focus your thinking on the specific area of competence you are considering. For example, the first item addresses the issue of taking time to listen before expressing your opinion. You may find that you do this adequately when you are dealing with people individually, but there are shortcomings when you are in a group situation (or vice-versa). Depending on what aspect of competence you are assessing, you may have different ratings.

In terms of rating your level of competence with respect to the forty items that are listed below, use the following scale to rate each item.

5 - Exceptional
4 - Fully satisfactory
3 - Adequate
2 - Requires some improvement
1 - Unsatisfactory

Rating
1. _____ take time to listen before expressing an opinion
2. _____ demonstrate a clear sense of direction
3. _____ think positively and am willing to take risks
4. _____ respect others
5. _____ use time efficiently and productively
6. _____ accept and learn from constructive criticism
7. _____ critically evaluate information
8. _____ consider all aspects of an issue
9. _____ communicate needs to persons in authority
10. _____ build positive relationships with others at all levels
11. _____ delegate tasks when it is appropriate

12. _____ approach new situations without undue apprehension
13. _____ clearly express ideas in writing
14. _____ demonstrate initiative when undertaking projects
15. _____ cope effectively with change
16. _____ take steps to keep up-to-date in key areas
17. _____ good understanding of basic concepts and specific facts
18. _____ maintain self control in conflict situations
19. _____ able to construe creative solutions to difficult problems
20. _____ act on the basis of long term plans
21. _____ seek out relevant information from a wide variety of sources
22. _____ perform tasks in an efficient manner
23. _____ willing to accept leadership responsibilities
24. _____ use knowledge of the system to overcome barriers and meet goals
25. _____ acquire additional information quickly and efficiently
26. _____ motivated and persistent when pursuing goals
27. _____ support and encourage others
28. _____ non-verbal gestures are consistent with verbal statements
29. _____ make sound judgments based on an understanding of the issues
30. _____ actions reflect a positive self image
31. _____ clearly express ideas in front of a group
32. _____ integrate personal goals and lifestyle with my work/education
33. _____ critically reflect upon performance and make changes according to observed results
34. _____ establish effective action plans
35. _____ able to adjust to organizational change
36. _____ effectively organize new information
37. _____ improve performance through questioning, observation and experience
38. _____ demonstrate flexibility when interpreting organizational guidelines
39. _____ provide others with constructive and positive feedback
40. _____ acknowledge my strengths and use my strength to good advantage

Scoring

The forty competence evaluation questions can be roughly divided into eight categories. The suggested order is listed below. Add the evaluations for each category together and derive a total score for each grouping.

A. **Purpose**	B. **Problem Solving**	C. **Communication Skills**
2. _____	8. _____	1. _____
14. _____	19. _____	13. _____
20. _____	21. _____	18. _____
26. _____	29. _____	28. _____
32. _____	34. _____	31. _____
Total: _____	Total: _____	Total: _____

D. **Theoretical Knowledge**	E. **Applied Knowledge**	F. **Organizational Adaptability**
1. _____	5. _____	6. _____
16. _____	15. _____	9. _____
20. _____	22. _____	24. _____
25. _____	33. _____	35. _____
36. _____	37. _____	38. _____
Total: _____	Total: _____	Total: _____

G. **Human Relations**	H. **Self Confidence**
4. _____	3. _____
10. _____	12. _____
11. _____	23. _____
27. _____	30. _____
30. _____	40. _____
Total: _____	Total: _____

About the Author

Norman Amundson, Ph.D. is a professor of counselling psychology in the Faculty of Education, University of British Columbia. He has over 20 years of experience as a counsellor educator and is currently editor of the Journal of Employment Counseling.

His publications include over 50 journal articles and several books, including the popular career books *Career Pathways* and *At the Controls: Charting Your Course Through Unemployment* (over 1 million in print).

Dr. Amundson is a regular conference presenter and has been a keynote speaker at international counselling conferences in Sweden, the United States, and Israel. He has presented training seminars and workshops in Canada, USA, Sweden, Denmark, Finland, Iceland, Hungary, Israel, New Zealand, Australia, and China.

As a consultant, Dr. Amundson has made significant contributions to Human Resources Development Canada (HRDC). He has played a key role in helping with the development of an employment counselling training program that has received both national and international acclaim. As part of a World Bank project, Dr. Amundson helped several universities in Hungary implement the HRDC training model as part of their counsellor training programs.

To Contact the Author

To contact Dr. Amundson:

Faculty of Education
University of British Columbia
Vancouver, B.C.   V6T 1Z4 Canada
Tel: (604) 822-6757   Fax: (604) 822-2328
E-mail: amundson@interchange.ubc.ca

To order *Active Engagement, Career Pathways, Career Pathways:Quick Trip, Employment counselling theory and strategies*, or other publications of Ergon Communications, contact:

Ergon Communications
3260 Springford Ave.
Richmond, B.C. V7E 1T9 Canada
Fax. (604) 448-9025